The FLORAL DECORATOR

KENNETH TURNER

Photographs by Marie-Louise Avery

Weidenfeld and Nicolson
London

First published in Britain in 1993 by
Weidenfeld and Nicolson
Orion Publishing Group
Orion House
5 Upper St Martin's Lane
London WC2H 9EA

ISBN 0 297 83230 1
CIP data for this book is available from the British Library.

Front jacket photographs Marie-Louise Avery
Back jacket photograph Kiloran Howard
All photographic credits and captions for prelims are on p. 159

.

Managing Editor Lesley Baxter
Design International Interiors

Phototypeset by Keyspools Ltd, Golborne, Lancs
Printed and bound in Italy

Editorial note   All linear measurements given in this book are for guidance only.
To convert approximately from imperial to metric multiply the stated figure by 2.5.

This book is dedicated to my sister Jill who, like myself, has had a love of flowers since childhood, and who at all times has encouraged me with her enthusiasm. It is also dedicated to the memory of our mother.

Floral decorating is to flower arranging
what painting is to colouring by numbers

C O N T

E N T S

FIRST PRINCIPLES

INTRODUCTION

Think of the last time you went for a woodland walk in spring and were surrounded by a dazzling sea of jostling bluebells. Think of a ramble down a country lane in summer or autumn and the wild profusion of flowers and fruits crowding the hedgerows, the trees rustling in the breeze. Or perhaps you wandered along a deserted beach and found pocketfuls of pebbles and strange-shaped pieces of driftwood.

Now consider the last time you saw a bunch of flowers in a vase – those drooping carnations in the middle of a restaurant table, that nice bowl of chrysanthemums hiding in the corner of a room. 'Nice' says it all, for such arrangements are flat, static, uninspiring to the beholder and, above all, unnatural. They use beautiful, natural materials and yet they're about as far from reflecting nature's beauty as you could possibly get.

Over the last thirty years, since I started work as a floral decorator, I have seen more 'nice' arrangements than I care to think about. Some of them have undoubtedly been created with a deal of skill, but the most important thing of all – imagination – is painfully conspicuous by its absence. No thought seems to have been given to the natural source from whence the flowers came. More than anything else, there seems to be scant respect for nature's inherent beauty.

A floral decoration should be a celebration of nature, reflecting all its colours, shapes, textures and spontaneous movement. It is the result of a combination of a few easily learned skills and imagination in abundance. The skills are straightforward to explain and demonstrate, as I hope to show here; imagination, I am convinced, can flourish by example. It can be developed in much the same way as someone who professes to be tone deaf can learn to sing in tune.

With a little practice and by listening, or in this case, observing, there first comes imitation and then the growth of individual style.

My aim is to explain the not so secret 'tricks' or techniques of a floral decorator's trade, and to show how I use them, combined with an appreciation and love of nature, to create my displays. My hope is that I will prove how simple the essential skills are and, most important of all, that some of my decorations may offer inspiration and trigger the imagination. Above all, I hope that after you have become familiar with the techniques and have experimented to discover your own style, your decorations will never be described by anyone as simply *nice*.

Roses, apples, blackberries, ivy, artichokes, lilies, hydrangeas – nature's beauty in abundance to fire the imagination. Whether you live in town or country, you will always be able to find a wide variety of materials from which to create decorations, if you keep both your eyes and mind open.

13

PLANNING A DISPLAY OR DECORATION

Planning any display, no matter how large or small, takes time and a great deal of thought. I realize I have just invited you to let your imagination run riot, and so you should, but there are a few very simple points to take into account first which, if anything, will help rather than hinder your creativity.

SETTING

Where are you going to put your display once you've finished it? No display should be conceived or prepared without some thought as to its surroundings, for the two should complement each other. Sometimes you may choose the setting first, in which case consider the space available, the decor and the style and colour of the furniture. At other times you may have the idea of a display in mind. Find the setting you think will be most appropriate and tailor the display to fit if necessary.

COLOUR

I remember planning a dinner-party decoration and being looked at askance by a colleague as I selected cerise under-plates and clashing deep red serviettes. When set on a rich blue cloth and decorated with pink, orange, red and white petals and flowers, however, the effect – as my colleague admitted – was stunning.

Choosing which colours to use in a display comes down very much to personal taste. I love clashing colours, but monochrome displays can look equally magnificent, particularly if set against dark green foliage. Experiment. Set different colours together and see whether they jar or complement each other. But remember one golden rule: always create pockets of colour in a display. Don't dither about sticking one red rose here, another there: the flowers

will lose all their impact and the overall effect will be a mess. Instead, arrange flowers of the same kind and colour in clusters for the richest, and most natural, effect.

TEXTURE

This is another important consideration. Try to incorporate materials with contrasting textures. Holly combined with larch and fir, for instance, looks

glorious in a Christmas decoration; a basket of hyacinths can be particularly eye-catching if a few broken pieces of terracotta pot are set underneath the plants.

SHAPE

By this I mean both the form of the decoration as a whole and the shapes of its constituent parts. A display should have a natural balance. If it looks too squat, add foliage or bare branches, for instance, to give it height; if it's too narrow, fronds of ivy or ferns will add width. And look for variety in the shapes of the materials you are using, arranging contrasting contours together to complement each other.

MOVEMENT

This is the most important point of all for, more than anything else, it distinguishes the 'nice', static display from the natural and spectacular. In large decorations, long branches or grasses can be used to break any rigid lines and create a natural look. With smaller displays, make sure there are no straight lines of colour *anywhere* and that the overall effect, while balanced, looks spontaneous and full of surprises.

As if these points weren't enough to think about all at once, there is one more vital consideration: the kind of container most appropriate for your decoration.

Broken pieces of terracotta pot set around the base of these hyacinths add natural colour, texture and shape to the display.

Never arrange one flower on its own in a display. Create pockets of colour by grouping the flowers in clusters. The effect will be both more vibrant and, above all, more natural.

CONTAINERS

The container used for a display should be regarded as an integral part of the design and chosen with as much thought as the other materials. All too often I have seen glorious decorations that have been let down by their pot, bowl, basket or urn. In itself the container may have looked superb, but employed as it was it was either out of proportion with the rest of the display, or the wrong shape or colour. It did not look as if it belonged to the rest of the display, nor the display to it.

I am often asked by clients to create a decoration for a particular container of theirs, which may be a huge, highly glazed urn or a delicate antique porcelain pot, a basket that has definitely seen better days, or a modern, perhaps rather severe, glass vase. In each case, not only has the final setting for the display to be taken into consideration, but also the container itself, if the overall effect is to be striking yet balanced. I might fill the urn with tall birch branches, whose height would balance the urn's width and whose rich colour and smooth texture would draw attention to the glaze. A porcelain pot could be decorated with a simple ball of dried marjoram, the basket covered with moss and filled with wild grasses, the vase packed with sand and shells with a shell sculpture on top.

The range of possibilities is, as ever, as wide as the imagination but, whether the idea for the display comes to you before you find a container, or whether you already have a cherished vessel that you wish to decorate, the two elements must make a unified whole.

It will come as no surprise to hear that I much prefer natural-looking containers to any other. Stone urns, terracotta pots and wicker baskets are immensely versatile and their texture and shaded colouring immediately adds interest to the entire display.

TERRACOTTA POTS

I don't use plastic 'terracotta' pots unless they are going to be hidden inside a more decorative container as their colour is completely flat. One wall in my studio, however, is covered in shelves full of proper terracotta pots in all sizes. No two are exactly alike, either in texture or shading, and the more worn and weathered they become, the more natural they look.

They are also much more versatile than brown plastic pots and can be stacked or screwed together so that they form not just an integral part of a decoration, but one of its main features.

Stacking pots Small pots can be stacked to make a very simple yet attractive candlestand (see p. 75); larger ones can be joined together, supported by moss and bamboo, for a tiered display.

● Take one large and one slightly smaller pot and fill the larger one three-quarters full with dry sack moss. Place the second

pot inside the first on top of the moss and push the bamboo cane through its drainage hole and into the moss below. Trim the cane so that it comes about halfway up the top pot.

The pots can now be decorated and used as a Christmas candlestand (see p. 154) or, if you use compost rather than moss, planted with herbs.

Screws and nuts Forget the times you cursed the drainage hole in the bottom of a pot as water ran out all over your feet and use the holes to attach two pots base to base with a screw and nut. Use this stand either as the central column in the pot herb and vegetable garden (see pp. 18–19) or for any pot display that requires added height.

A container should be an integral part of the design, complementing the other materials in size, colour and texture. In this dried arrangement of hydrangeas, marjoram, wheat and poppy heads, the pots and urn are as subtly shaded and natural-looking as the flowers, and their combined height allows the broad expanse of wheat to be displayed to full effect.

*This **terracotta pot herb and vegetable garden** (pp. 18–19) is made from a few readily available materials and would make a glorious natural display – if visitors could be persuaded not to nibble at the tomatoes and mushrooms.*

TERRACOTTA POT HERB AND VEGETABLE GARDEN

Tools and materials

- glue gun
- circular piece of chipboard – I used a piece measuring about 18 inches in diameter. Alternatively, you could use an old circular tray.
- about 25 terracotta pots in various sizes, no smaller than 3 inches and no larger than 7 inches across
- screws
- nuts
- stub wire
- dry sack moss
- carpet moss
- house plant compost
- selection of miniature vegetables and fresh herbs, such as cherry tomatoes, mushrooms, turnip, broccoli, garden peas, aubergines, red cauliflower, rosemary, thyme, basil, parsley
- bunches of carrots complete with their tops (optional)

Method

• Cover one side and the edge of the board with carpet moss, sticking it down with glue. If you are using a tray, invert it and stick the moss to the base and around the lip.

• Take the two largest pots and join them base to base with a screw and washer (see p. 16). Then set them in the centre of the board or tray and glue securely to the moss.

• Arrange pairs of smaller pots around the centre, again screwing them together base to base, and set the remaining pots one by one around the edge of the board. Try several arrangements until you find the one that looks the most balanced and then glue all the pots in place.

• Set the vegetables and herbs in the pots. The aim is a look of natural abundance, so arrange them to give the greatest contrasts in colour, texture and shape. The peas, turnip, broccoli, aubergines and cauliflower need no support and can be placed in any pot you choose; the herbs should be planted in compost or, if they have come in their own pots, transferred to the display complete with their soil. Fill the pots that are to hold the tomatoes and mushrooms with dry sack moss and pile the vegetables on top. Use a piece of stub wire to attach to the moss any that persist in rolling off.

• If you want to create a truly glorious indoor garden, set the display on a table or dresser covered with a protective cloth or piece of polythene and surround it with more carpet moss and bunches of carrots complete with their feathery green tops.

POT AND BIRCH POLE STANDS

I love the natural, flickering light of candles and always use them at home for parties. I also very often prepare candlestands for clients, for what better way to do justice to the gentle glow of a candle flame than to make a stand from natural materials? Here, again, terracotta pots come into their own, because with a little preparation they are the ideal container for a birch pole stand – the trusty base for a host of candle decorations.

PREPARING A BIRCH POLE CANDLESTAND

● Take a piece of birch pole and drill a hole in one end to hold the candle. The pole can be any length you like, although 12–18 inches is ideal, and should be wide enough to allow half an inch all round the hole, which should be at least $1\frac{1}{2}$ inches deep to support the candle.

● Find a terracotta pot large enough to support your pole without toppling over. Don't use a pot if it is cracked or has an uneven base as there must be no risk of the pot falling apart when the candle is lit, or of it wobbling or, worse, falling over.

● Next, fix the pole in the pot. The most secure way to do this is to use finishing plaster or light cement which, when set, will hold the pole firmly in position. First, line the pot with polythene. This not only seals the drainage hole but allows the plaster or cement to expand – which it does as it hardens – without sticking to the pot sides and cracking the terracotta. Mix up the plaster or cement following the manufacturer's instructions and pour it into the pot until it is about half full.

Push the pole into the centre of the cement and leave to harden.

● When the plaster or cement has set and the pole is held firmly, it can be used to make any number of decorated candlestands (see opposite, pp. 42, 63, 74, 94, 101).

● To fit the candle securely, simply wedge it into the hole in the top of the pole. If it is loose, straighten it and fix it in position with Oasis Fix.

Pot and pole stands can also be used for large displays, such as free-standing wedding altar pieces (see pp. 118–19), or for the topiary orange 'tree' described pp. 148–9. In such instances you'll need a large bowl or bucket rather than a pot, the poles will be longer, and you'll need considerably more plaster or cement – but the principle is just the same!

BOX CANDLESTAND

Tools and materials

- scissors
- drill with $1\frac{1}{2}$-inch bit
- terracotta pot large enough to support the pole and candle
- polythene to line the pot
- 12-inch birch pole
- finishing plaster or light cement
- reel wire
- branches of box cut into 3-inch lengths
- 12-inch long, $1\frac{1}{2}$-inch diameter candle

Method

- Drill a $1\frac{1}{2} \times 1\frac{1}{2}$-inch hole in one end of the pole.
- Prepare the birch pole stand as described opposite.
To cover the pole with the sprigs of box (again, this uses a procedure that can be widely applied when attaching any flower or foliage to a pole)
- Wind reel wire around the top of the pole four or five times so that it is firmly attached and then let the reel drop to the work surface.
- Take a handful of box and, making sure the leaves are pointing upwards and that it is evenly spread, hold it firmly around the top of the pole.
- Pick up the reel wire and tightly bind it round the lower ends of the box stalks.

- Once the first layer of box is wired to the pole, take another handful and bind it in in the same way, making sure the reel wire of the layer above is completely hidden. There is no need to tie off the wire every time you finish a layer — if it is wound tightly enough it will hold one layer in place while you prepare the next.
- Work your way down the pole, binding in the box, until you reach the base and plaster. Wrap the wire round two or three times and tie it off.
- Cover the top of the cement with moss and there you are — you have your first candlestand.

BASKETS

Baskets come in an almost limitless variety of shapes and sizes. And just because they may look as if they've stepped out of a country garden does not mean they have to be confined to holding displays of dried flowers, grasses and herbs, although these can look stunning. Properly prepared, baskets can be used for a host of decorations, from profuse displays of fresh flowers to sculpted decorations of bound branches.

Baskets can also be covered very easily and to great effect, so don't throw away any that look as if they've seen better days – cover them with fir cones, hessian, rope or moss and give them a new lease of life.

COVERING BASKETS

Hessian Take a square or rectangular piece of hessian big enough to cover the base and sides of the basket, lay it out flat and place the basket in the centre. Pull up the corners of the hessian to the basket rim and, holding each firmly, bind with a length of florist's wire. Once all four corners are secured, conceal the wire with rope or raffia bows.

Rope binding Stand the basket on a flat surface, secure one end of a length of rope with reel wire to a point on the basket rim and slowly coil the rope round the basket until you reach the base. Having made sure there are no gaps in the binding, fasten the loose end of rope with reel wire to the bottom of the basket, above the base. Then take more reel wire and, attaching it to the basket rim and working vertically to the base, 'sew' the rope to the wickerwork. Pull the wire tightly as you go to give a 'woven' effect and then securely tie it off.

Fir cones These look particularly attractive on baskets used for Christmas decorations. Gather as many cones as you think you'll need to cover your basket and wire them up one at a time (see p. 26). Starting at the basket rim and working round and down, wire the cones to the wickerwork until it is completely covered.

Moss The rich colour and velvety texture of carpet moss can revive the oldest of baskets. Trim off any loose ends of wickerwork that would otherwise pierce the moss covering, take some dry carpet moss and simply glue it to the basket's exterior, including the handle if there is one.

Whether or not the outside of a basket is decorated, its inside will always need preparation.

PREPARING BASKETS FOR DISPLAYS

By protecting the inside of a basket with polythene or plastic bin liner, it can be used again and again without being damaged.

- Take a piece of polythene that will cover the basket's inside and press it down flat across the base and up the side, making folds as necessary so that it fits snugly. Trim the polythene to stand above the basket rim by about an inch, then fold the excess under, making a neat 'hem'. Then staple the lining to the wickerwork around the basket rim.

As well as a plastic lining, I always put a bowl inside the basket, even for dried displays – it doesn't take much for a sharp stalk or wire to pierce the polythene, and all your work will have been wasted.

Properly prepared, baskets can be used for a host of decorations. Fill small ones with pot-pourri to adorn a dressing table; stand bound birch branches in a larger one for an arresting hallway display. A flat basket with a handle can make a conversation-stopping party piece: simply bind tall grasses or wheat stalks, fresh herbs and a few seasonal flowers with reel wire to the sides of the handle, fill the basket tray with tempting canapés or fruit and offer it round.

WIRE, AND MOSS AND WIRE MOULDS

Most displays need support of some kind to show the natural ingredients to best advantage. The traditional method is to use an oasis ball or ring and while I don't eschew these at all, I prefer netting, or sack moss and netting moulds, using 2-inch chicken wire.

PREPARING A WIRE MOULD

These are used for fresh displays that require water. The size of the piece of netting will obviously depend on the size of the bowl, but as a guide, a piece 36 inches by 18 is about right for a 12-inch diameter bowl.

● Lay the wire out flat and slowly and methodically bend it firmly but not too tightly into a ball. There will be loose (and sharp) ends down one and possibly two sides of the wire, which should be wrapped over complete strands in the netting, not only to secure the mould but also for safety and neatness. The finished ball should be rigid, evenly shaped and have plenty of holes large enough to hold clusters of flowers.

● Fit the ball into a bowl and secure it in place. Tie a length of reel wire to the mould at a point near the bowl rim, feed the wire down and under the bowl and attach it to the mould on the other side. Turn the bowl and mould 90° and repeat.

Once the bowl is filled with water, you can begin to prepare your display. This is the most testing time: if the ball is too loosely shaped, it will not support the flowers as they are inserted; if it is too dense, the stalks may well split or snap as they are pushed in. In either case, the only remedy is to take the ball apart and re-mould it, but get it right once and you've mastered the technique for ever.

PREPARING MOSS AND WIRE MOULDS

I use these for dried displays and also for garlands or swags wired with materials of all kinds. When making a dried display, use dry sack moss otherwise the flower stalks or grasses will rot; use damp sack moss to support fresh flowers and foliage.

The procedure is much the same as for a wire mould.

● First (see 1 OPPOSITE), take a length of wire, lay it out flat and place four or five large handfuls of sack moss down the centre. Arrange the moss in an even strip, teasing out all the lumps as you go.

● That done, bend the wire around the moss, rolling the strip into a ball as you do so (see 2 OPPOSITE). Turn in all loose ends of wire as described above.

● Once the ball is complete, fit it into a pot or bowl and secure it with reel wire. The bowl can then be placed in a pre-lined basket. Adjust the mould if necessary to create a smooth dome (see 3 OPPOSITE).

The mould is now ready for decoration (see 4 OPPOSITE). Again, it is only now that you'll know whether the mould is the right density or whether you will have to unwind it and start again!

MOULDS FOR GARLANDS OR SWAGS

● Make a moss and wire mould just as you would if you were filling a bowl, remembering to use dry moss to hold dried ingredients, damp for fresh materials. Instead of rolling the wire and moss into a ball, however, simply shape it into a long strip about 10 inches wide, folding the edges of wire around the moss and bending the loose ends over complete strands in the netting to make the mould secure. This is now ready for decoration (see pp. 28–9), after which it should be backed with protective polythene (see left).

The back of a garland or swag should always be lined with a piece of polythene or plastic bin liner to protect the surface against which it is to be hung. Once the garland is decorated – don't line it beforehand in case wires or stalks pierce the plastic as they are inserted – simply take a length of polythene and attach it with stub wire or hair pins, folding the edges in neatly.

1

2

3

4

WIRING MATERIALS FOR DISPLAYS

Fresh and dried flowers, fruits, vegetables, nuts, shells and even small terracotta pots can all be wired and incorporated into displays to create a riot of natural colours, shapes, textures and movement.

FLOWERS

The only materials you will need are a pair of scissors and lengths of strong florist's wire. Remember that the aim is to group flowers of the same kind and colour into vibrant clusters, so unless they are very large there is no need to wire them up individually.

● Take 3 or more flowers, depending on their size, and trim the stems to about 3 inches.

● Strip off any leaves that will get in the way of the wire and firmly clasp the stalks together in one hand.

● Take a length of florist's wire and, with the same hand, tightly hold one end of it against the stalks. With your free hand, wind the wire firmly round the stalks three or four times and twist the two ends of wire together.

FRUIT AND VEGETABLES

Since these are relatively heavy, I tend to wire them up individually and often use two lengths of wire at a time.

● To wire an apple or pepper, for instance, hold it base upwards and push

the wires through about a third of the way up from the bottom. Pull the ends of the wires together underneath and twist together.

NUTS AND CONES

These should be wired one by one but, depending on their size, can be grouped afterwards by twisting their wires together.

● To attach a wire to a nut, make a small hole in the shell near the base using a bradawl. Push the wire into the nut as far as it will go and then glue around the hole to keep the wire in place.

Fir cones, by comparison, are extremely easy to wire up as long as they are sufficiently open.

● Simply feed a length of wire around

the cone near its base, pull the wire ends together and twist into a stalk.

SHELLS

Many small shells do not need wiring into a display – they can simply be glued on.

● To prepare larger shells, such as scallops, drill two small holes about an inch apart near the shell's base. Feed a length of wire through the holes and twist together.

TERRACOTTA POTS

Small pots look wonderful when wired into displays.

● Once again, the drainage hole comes in handy because all you have to do is pass a piece of wire through it and up and over

the pot side, and then wind the two ends together.

● Should there be no drainage hole, either drill a hole in the base, or through the pot from side to side, and wire up as usual.

Many other materials can be wired up, including small baskets, short birch poles bound with rope, cinammon stick bundles tied with raffia . . . the list is as long as your imagination allows it to be.

OVERLEAF *Garlands wired with fresh flowers, fruit, vegetables or dried materials of all kinds make glorious decorations. They can be any length you like, but even a short, 5-foot one will use up a surprisingly large quantity of materials, so plan carefully. They do not need to be reserved for special occasions, but can be*

hung around the home as an alternative to a large container display.

*From left to right: this **rose garland** (pp. 28–9) shows just how simple and serene an effect can be achieved by using just two types of rose in complementary colours.*

By comparison, the multi-coloured clusters of roses, lilies, amaryllis, rosemary, black grapes and red apples exude nothing but wild exuberance.

Garlands of dried materials make an eye-catching permanent decoration full of many shapes and textures. Below the 'sheaf' of wheat at the top of the dried flower garland cascade roses, peonies, terracotta pots filled with moss, poppy heads, lavender, citrus fruits and marjoram.

As a complete change, and yet still using nothing but the most natural of materials, these subtly coloured and multi-shaped shells look magnificent when wired in groups and set against the rich red-brown of eucalyptus fronds.

CARPET MOSS AND FRESH ROSE GARLAND

Tools and materials

- scissors
- glue gun
- polythene or plastic bin liner to back garland
- 2-inch wire netting
- stub wire or hair pins
- florist's wire
- damp sack moss
- carpet moss
- birch branches (optional)
- small and medium-sized roses in two complementary colours

Method

- Prepare the moss and wire garland mould (see p. 24).

- Take pieces of carpet moss and pin them to the front and sides of the garland with stub wire or hair pins. I don't cover every garland with carpet moss before I wire in the other materials, but in this case it gives a particularly rich, velvety texture against which to display the roses.

- Trim the stalks of the roses to about 3 inches and keep the remainder to one side, then wire the flowers together in small groups (see p. 26).

- Starting at one end of the garland, wire in a row of roses of one colour and then a row of the other, making sure that only the stalks and not the wires are visible, but allowing a little of the carpet moss to show through.

- Work your way down the garland, alternating the colours until the mould is completely covered.

- Wire together groups of the rose stems that you have kept to one side and insert these into the top of the garland in a fan shape.

- Conceal the stem ends either by covering them with more roses or by making a birch and moss bow. Take the supple birch branches and bind them into a bow shape, using more branches or wire to hold it in position. Stick carpet moss all over the bow with glue, thread a piece of wire across the back and attach it to the garland round the rose stems.

- Finally, pin the protective polythene to the back of the garland (see p. 24).

INGREDIENTS FOR DISPLAYS

I know I'm stating the obvious, but it is worth emphasizing that a decoration, even if it is created with skill and imagination, will be a disappointment if it is not made of the best of ingredients. No amount of creative arrangement, judicious choice of container or clever piece of wiring will ever disguise the wilting flower, bruised apple, tired-looking dried spray or chipped shell.

FRESH FLOWERS

I make a point of using nothing but the freshest of fresh flowers and, after thirty years in the business, still go to market every morning to pick the best from amongst a sea of bunches, both for the

shop and for clients' displays. If I know I have a decoration to create for a particular function, then I buy the flowers a day or two in advance, picking them when they are still closed to give them time to open and be at their most spectacular at the appointed time.

I recommend, therefore, that you 'cultivate' a friendship with the local florist. (You can, of course, use flowers from the garden, but you'd be surprised how many you need to create a really large display, and why spoil an area you have carefully tended?) Find a good florist, one who stocks a wide variety of flowers, and don't be afraid to ask if there's something specific that you want – they'll probably be only too happy to

oblige and will come to regard you as a kindred spirit.

One last point, however. The florist may look at you with some surprise if you regularly ask for flowers out of season – daffodils in September, for instance, or polyanthus in October, holly in June. It's not that they will be unwilling to find them for you, it's just that it may strike them as an odd – and expensive – way to create displays.

The above examples are extremes, but I feel very strongly that consideration of the seasons and the flowers that grow in each is absolutely essential to creating a truly natural display. A decoration should pay respect to nature and if nature dictates that daffodils grow in springtime and holly in the winter, I will plan my displays accordingly.

The result, of course, is that there are months of the year when seasonal fresh flowers are more difficult to find. Don't abandon the idea of making decorations, but use the opportunity to experiment with dried flowers, or branches, or shells and driftwood.

People often say to me, 'I bought some fresh flowers only two days ago and already they've wilted.' The point is that, unless they've been kept by a radiator and starved of water, they probably weren't that fresh. I replenish the fresh flowers in the shop every day with new ones brought straight from market. Using the freshest of flowers in displays is the only way to guarantee that the display will last a reasonable time and that all your hard work will not have been wasted.

*For me, this **basket of hyacinths** (p. 34–5) is the perfect evocation of spring and is something I would therefore only make at the beginning of the year. Come the autumn and winter, my mind would naturally turn to creating displays using materials such as blackberries, hawthorn, hollies, fir cones or juniper and larch.*

A FRESH SPRING BASKET

Tools and materials

- scissors
- staple gun
- large shallow basket
- polythene to line basket
- plastic bowl that fits snugly inside the basket
- length of 2-inch wire netting
- reel wire
- carpet moss
- narcissi
- white hyacinths
- lauristinus

Method

- Line the basket with polythene, stapling it to the rim (see p. 23).

- Make a wire mould to fit the plastic bowl (see p. 24), remembering to tie the mould in place with reel wire.

- Put the bowl in the basket and fill in around the edge with carpet moss to hide both the rim and any of the basket's polythene lining.

- Fill the bowl with water to within an inch and a half of the top and then simply arrange first the narcissi, then the hyacinths and finally the lauristinus using the wire mould as a support. The display must look natural, though, so arrange the narcissi in clusters, never singly, and never in straight lines.

FRUIT AND VEGETABLES

In addition to fresh flowers, consider the variety of colours, shapes and textures provided by introducing fruit and vegetables to a display. You can find a basketful just by walking round your local supermarket – perhaps that's why they are so often overlooked: they are taken for granted and their natural beauty is simply forgotten.

Apples, oranges, lemons, pomegranates, melons, grapes all look superb when wired into a garland or large basket display (see p. 146). I often use them in Christmas decorations when there are fewer seasonal flowers available.

Aubergines, cauliflower, ornamental cabbage, red and yellow peppers all add striking splashes of colour and sometimes a slightly irreverent note to the most formal of decorations.

HERBS

These, too, are often overlooked, but there could be nothing more natural than a selection of small herb pots 'planted' in moss down the centre of a rustic-looking kitchen table, or the herb and vegetable garden described on pp. 18–19.

Rosemary is a particular favourite of mine and I use it in decorations ranging from bridal headdresses to formal candlestands, not just because of its attractive shape and texture but also because of its scent, which adds an extra dimension to any display. The sculpted rosemary pots pictured and described here will be an instant conversation piece – you need not let on how very simple they are to make!

TOPIARY ROSEMARY POT

Tools and materials

- scissors
- glue gun
- terracotta pot
- foam ball that will sit in the top of the pot
- fresh rosemary – the quantity will depend on the size of your pot and ball, and you'll need sprigs with both a feathery end and woody stalk

Method

• Cut the woodier stalks of the rosemary into lengths the height of the pot, then glue them on all the way round.

• Glue round the inside edge of the pot and press the foam ball in place so that it sits securely.

• Take the feathery sprigs of rosemary and cut them into 3-inch lengths. Then simply stick these into the foam ball until it is completely covered.

• Trim the ball all over to give a sculpted, topiary effect, but only cut off a little rosemary at a time – trim it too severely and before you know it you'll be left with nothing but the foam ball again in an attempt to create an even shape.

DRIED FLOWERS

When I first started as a floral decorator, using dried flowers was virtually unheard of. Today, however, you can't walk past any florist's without seeing dried displays, and even my local post office sells dainty (if rather predictable) dried baskets around Mother's Day.

With so many sources of dried flowers now available, it is very easy to create impressive displays with the minimum of fuss. You can, however, dry your own very easily, which can be an added source

of pride when someone compliments your displays. Dried arrangements, though, use even more flowers than large fresh displays, so use your friendly florist again as a source, rather than strip your garden bare.

DRYING FLOWERS

The best place to dry flowers is somewhere warm, well-ventilated and dark. Here, the flowers will dry quickly before they spoil or fade. An airing cupboard is ideal, but an attic or

understairs cupboard will serve equally well as long as it is not damp. Most flowers will dry perfectly if hung upside down and suspended on a hook or wire in the traditional manner.

The time a flower takes to dry depends very much on its size, on whether it's hung with others or on its own, and on the temperature and ventilation of the drying area. Small roses hung in bunches of 5 to 7 in a dark airing cupboard should be dry within three or four days, but there are no hard and fast rules. The only

important thing to check is that the flowers are completely dry right down to their heads before you bring them out and use them in displays.

TIPS ON PICKING AND DRYING

● The best time to pick flowers for drying is when they are at or immediately before their best.

● Don't pick wet flowers if you can help it. If you do have flowers with soaking petals, leave them in a vase of water until the moisture has evaporated from the flower head before you hang them up to dry.

● Flowers broken from their stems by wind or rain can be hung up to dry, even if they have not opened. Once dry, hold the head over a gently steaming pot or kettle and slowly open the petals as they moisten, making sure that the outer ones do not become so wet that they drop off. Once open, leave to dry again before using them in a display.

Clusters of vibrantly coloured dried flowers can be used to create displays that will adorn a room all year round. Such displays also require very little attention compared with the fresh decoration that needs regular watering.

Balls of dried flowers make arresting table decorations when grouped together. Make a dry moss and wire mould (see p. 24) that will sit snugly on top of a terracotta pot. Cut the dried flower stems to within 2 inches of the flower head and simply insert them into the ball until it is completely covered.

SHELLS, DRIFTWOOD AND OTHER NATURAL MATERIALS

I have, for a long time now, used much more than the obvious materials of a florist's trade in my decorations. I look at everything nature provides and that includes the treasure-trove of shells, bits of driftwood and curiously shaped pebbles to be found on the seashore. Their colours, shapes and textures never cease to amaze me and all can be incorporated very easily and to stunning effect into displays for all situations and occasions.

● For instance, fill a tall glass vase with layers of sand and small pebbles.

● Make a dry sack moss and wire mould (see p. 24) to fit the top of the vase and attach a multiplicity of wired shells (see p. 27), starfish and sea urchins.

● Just when it looks as if you could not find space for one more item, glue tiny shells to the larger ones to give an impression of true natural abundance.

Alternatively, you might choose a much more simple yet equally stunning look.

● Fill an unadorned, shallow glass bowl or tray with pebbles of various sizes and plant tall flowers, such as amaryllis, amongst them. The effect is one of supreme grace and elegance – and it's so easy to create!

● Or dig out an old basket you thought would never be used again and wire large shells to the outside of the wickerwork. Fill the gaps between the shells with lichen moss stuck down with a little glue and pile the basket high with driftwood and pebbles.

A word of caution, though. Displays like these can be very heavy, so either make them *in situ* or have someone on hand to help you lift them once completed.

The next time you walk along the seashore, look out for shells, pebbles and curiously shaped pieces of driftwood. It's all too easy to dismiss them as lumps in the sand, but once collected and cleaned they can be used in any number of displays. Sea urchins, starfish, crabs and other sea creatures can readily be acquired from local craft shops.

*A **shell candlestand** (pp. 42–3) makes an arresting table or dresser centrepiece, the candle, once lit, picking out the subtlest details in the shells and lichen moss.*

SHELL CANDLESTAND

Tools and materials

- scissors
- glue gun
- drill with $1\frac{1}{2}$-inch bit
- terracotta pot large enough to support the pole and candle
- polythene to line the pot
- 12-inch birch pole
- finishing plaster or light cement
- length of 1-inch wire netting to cover the pole
- stub wire
- reel wire
- lichen moss
- 3×12-inch pre-strung shell necklaces
- 30 or so assorted shells
- 8 starfish (optional)
- 6 seahorses (optional)
- 12-inch long, $1\frac{1}{2}$-inch diameter candle

Method

- Drill a $1\frac{1}{2} \times 1\frac{1}{2}$-inch hole in one end of the pole.

- Prepare the birch pole stand as described on p. 20.

- Fill the top of the pot with lichen moss, pushing it in around the pole to hide the plaster or cement.

- Glue small tufts of lichen moss to the pole so that it is covered evenly all over, then wrap the wire netting firmly round the pole, over the moss. Overlap the wire edges by about an inch and bind them together with twists of stub wire.

- Take a shell necklace and wire one end to the moss and wire pole with reel wire, starting at the top. Wind the string round and down the pole, securing it to the netting in two or three pieces with short lengths of reel wire. Don't cover the pole completely, but leave spaces as you wind so that the moss, with its attractive colour and texture, can still be seen. Continue to attach the necklaces in this way, starting each new one where the preceding one finished, until you reach the pole base. Attach the loose end to the pole with reel wire as before and trim as necessary.

- Starting again at the top of the pole, glue the loose shells, starfish and seahorses to the small necklace shells. Spread them evenly but, as before, leave space for the moss to show through.

- Wedge the candle firmly in its hole, securing it with Oasis Fix if it wobbles.

TIPS AND PRECAUTIONS

• A decoration should not be seen in isolation from its surroundings, so look at the setting before you begin any display, and plan accordingly.

• Remember the key words 'colour', 'texture', 'shape', 'movement'.

• Gather together all the tools and materials required for a display before you start.

• Choose a container for a decoration as carefully as you would choose the other materials you are going to use.

• Always line baskets with protective polythene and set a bowl or other water-tight container inside.

• Back moss and wire garlands with polythene to protect the surface against

which they are to be hung.

• Use damp moss for fresh displays; dry moss for those containing dried materials.

• Use only the freshest of fresh flowers and plants.

• Remember the seasons and use those flowers that are readily available at any given time. Your decorations will not only be less expensive to make, but will also look more appropriate.

• When making decorations for a particular event, buy fresh, closed flowers a day or two in advance to give them time to open and look their best when the appointed time comes.

I have no wish to sound dictatorial, nor to be accused of stating the obvious, but:

• Keep all tools and materials, such as scissors, staple guns, glue guns, saws, drills, pieces of wire, polythene bags, broken pots, plaster or cement powder, safely out of the reach of children.

• When preparing candlestands using terracotta pots, make sure:
  the candle support is firmly held in place with cement or moss
  the pot is large enough to support the total height of the stand and candle
  the pot base is flat so that the whole thing will not fall over.
  the candle sits securely in position, made fast with Oasis Fix if necessary.

• Never leave a lit candle unattended and make sure the flame is kept away from all combustible materials.

• Never hang or mount a garland or display so close to a hearth with an open fire that it could be set alight by a spark or falling log or coal.

• If you are preparing any large, free-standing display, make sure its base is flat, that it is not top-heavy and that it will stand absolutely steady, even when people walk past.

These tulips may not look much more than a sea of green at the moment, but in twenty-four hours they will have opened into a mass of colour to grace the 50 tables at a client's party.

Drills, scissors, sticks or poles with sharp ends should be confined to the workbench and stored away when not in use, polythene bags – and their contents – stashed well out of harm's way.

A HOME FULL OF FLOWERS

A home bereft of flowers is, to me, barely a home at all. For nothing brings a home to life in quite the same way as a natural decoration, be it of fresh or dried flowers, fruit, herbs, shells or driftwood. Moreover, given the enormous variety of materials available, I believe that decorations, if carefully planned, can be created for any home, however large or small, however formal or informal its style.

In some ways, the home is the easiest place to practise your skills as a floral decorator, because you can experiment in private until you're confident of your technique. Also, being as familiar as you are with your surroundings, it will be that much easier to create decorations in a style to suit.

This familiarity, though, can sometimes be more of a hindrance than a help when it comes to letting your imagination have a free rein, for at first glance a room setting may preclude a particular idea you have in mind for a display – there may not be enough space, for instance, or the table you want to decorate is in the wrong place. Stand back and look at the setting as if for the first time. Imagine the room without any furniture at all, or picture it with the furniture rearranged. If you then discover new spaces that would be ideal for a decoration, or find that a table is the perfect place for a decoration if moved from one part of the room to another, change things around!

PREVIOUS PAGE *Every room in my house contains a decoration of some kind, each created from the materials most appropriate for the setting; each designed to make best use of the space available. In my basement living room, for instance, two dried displays fill a far wall which receives little natural light.*
Outside in the garden fresh foliage brought straight from market lies waiting while I prepare the container for a decoration of simple Spring greenery (see pp. 50–1).

FRESH DECORATIONS

While they do not last as long as dried decorations, there is nothing like a display of fresh, seasonal flowers and foliage to bring a room to life. The procedure for preparing any fresh display is very simple and is the same, whatever flowers or foliage you are using.

- First, find a container that is appropriate both for the display you have in mind and the final setting. If the display is to be a large one, I'd recommend you make it *in situ* as a large urn or pot full of water and cascading flowers is heavy and difficult to move.

- If the container is not watertight, line it with a plastic bowl. Then firmly wedge a wire mould (see p. 24) in the centre and fill with water.

- Give the decoration its height and width before filling in the centre. Take the flowers or foliage with the longest stems and insert them into the top and around the edges of the mould. In the example illustrated here, fronds of ivy give the decoration its depth, width and also its movement, branches of birch its height.

- Fill the remainder of the mould, grouping flowers of the same type and colour into clusters and juxtaposing contrasting shapes and texture. In this display, the bold heads of dill are set against delicate weeping birch; euphorbia, viburnum and sorbus all add subtle shading; and, in the centre, smooth, shining crowns of magnolia grandiflora highlight the many textures behind, 'cleaning up' the whole display.

The refreshing colours in these two decorations (ABOVE) are accentuated in very different ways. In one, supple, slender spring branches are bound with rough string over and around the base of the plants into a frame that immediately leads the eye to the delicately coloured blooms it surrounds. In the other, the vibrant colours are quite strong enough to catch the eye without any help. Instead, to complement them, to make more of a feature of the trusty terracotta pot, and to add unexpected texture, I simply bound the pot in rust-coloured rope.

As an alternative to the fresh-water displays just described, simple decorations of flowers planted in soil can be equally effective and have the advantage that, with minimal tending, they last much longer.

Consider the rows of potted plants you might have lined up waiting to be transferred to the garden when the weather is warmer. If they're already flowering, it would be the greatest waste to leave them crowded together in that back room when they could be brought out and displayed in all their splendour.

Alternatively, your florist will undoubtedly have a wide range of pre-potted seasonal flowers that, with the minimum of fuss, could be transformed from a 'nice' arrangement into a stylish, natural decoration. Look beyond what might appear to be just a pot full of flowers and, bearing in mind what I've said before about shape, colour, and the importance of the container itself to the overall effect, add your own finishing touches. Then place it in your chosen setting, or make a gift of it to a friend or relative.

OPPOSITE *The height and texture of these cheering spring hyacinths are emphasized and complemented merely by inserting varying lengths of slender birch branches all around the edge of the pot. The rich colour of the branches immediately draws attention to what might otherwise be just another 'nice' arrangement, and their shape and texture contrasts with and sets off the main feature of the decoration — the hyacinth heads with their many furling petals.*

Later in the year, when late spring frosts are long gone, this jasmine may well be planted in the garden. Before then, while it is still 'housebound', its profusion of delicate flowers will grace any well-lit, airy corner and fill the room with their scent. To highlight the plant's rampant growth, I surrounded it with a light bamboo frame, whose structural lines act as a foil to the tendril-like stems that will shoot in all directions, heedless of any attempt to bring them under control.

DRIED DECORATIONS

Over the last few years, with the increasing availability of dried flowers, decorations of dried materials of all kinds have become a common sight in many a home. And for good reason, for not only are the materials readily available, but dried displays are long-lasting, require minimal or no maintenance and can be used in areas – dark corners, high up on walls – where fresh displays would quickly fade or be difficult to maintain.

You can always spot them, though, those baskets of drieds that looked pretty in the shop, but which were bought more for convenience than anything else. Since little thought will have been given as to where they were going to be placed once back at home, they invariably lose all their charm and become nothing more than: 'something-I-spotted-by-accident-but-which-will-fill-a-hole', rather than a decoration chosen not just because it was attractive but also because it was appropriate. Since dried decorations are usually intended to be on display for some time it is, if anything, more important than ever to consider their setting.

At the risk of repeating myself, it's also vital to consider colour, shape, texture and movement when creating a dried decoration, and to do so while bearing in mind one very important point: though vibrant, these materials have by their nature none of the spontaneity of fresh flowers. You will therefore have to compensate. When grouping flowers into clusters, you will almost certainly have to use a larger quantity than you would if the same flowers had been fresh. Five medium-sized fresh roses wired together will provide a splash of colour that will be nothing more than an insignificant dot with no impact if the same number of the same flower had been wired when dry.

Shapes and textures, too, have to be

looked at anew, the relatively sharp, brittle forms softened by careful selection and juxtaposition.

Drieds come into their own when used to decorate dark or inaccessible areas where fresh flowers would quickly fade or be difficult to maintain.
ABOVE *Balls of dried marjoram set in delicate porcelain pots complement the subtle decor of a client's windowless hallway, while underneath stands a basket of dried hydrangeas, their large heads adding that all-important element of surprise, as well as additional colour and texture.*
OPPOSITE TOP RIGHT *This table base, created for a glass-topped coffee table, would have been impossible to make with fresh flowers. The central pillar is made of birch poles bound and nailed together (a word of caution: allow the*

poles to dry out completely before setting the glass on top or, if they are not dry, allow air to circulate by supporting the glass on short, transparent plastic stilts, otherwise the tops of the poles will go mouldy). Around the poles is a dried garland of roses, hydrangeas, marjoram, rosemary and wheat – an unusual, eye-catching decoration that requires no maintenance at all.

This **basket of dried wheat** (p. 56) and **larkspur and lavender sheaf** (p. 57) adorn the walls of a client's kitchen. Set above the wall units, they are displayed to full effect and immediately draw the eye; they also complement the room as a whole by emphasizing its height and by filling an area that would normally be dismissed as 'the space above the cupboards'.

BASKET OF DRIED WHEAT

Tools and materials

- scissors
- basket
- 2-inch wire netting
- florist's wire
- dry sack moss
- raffia or rough string
- dried ingredients: wheat, grasses, poppy heads, lavender, marjoram, artichokes, strings of peppers

Method

• Make a wire netting mould (see p. 24) and set it in the basket, attaching it to the rim in two or three places with florist's wire. On this occasion, since all the ingredients are dried, there's no need to line the basket unless you think any of the stalks might damage the wickerwork.

• Fill the netting mould with dried wheat.

• Then make a dry sack moss and wire netting garland support (see p. 24) that will fit round the basket rim.

• Wire up small bunches of grasses, poppy heads, lavender and marjoram, covering the wire binding with raffia or string; then wire the artichokes individually.

• Cover one side of the garland with the wired materials and then wrap it round the rim of the basket, binding its ends together and securing it to the wickerwork in three or four places with short lengths of florist's wire. Lastly, drape strings of peppers around the materials in the garland to add final splashes of colour.

SHEAF OF LARKSPUR AND LAVENDER

Tools and materials

- scissors
- staple gun
- piece of chipboard measuring about 24 × 24 inches
- 2-inch wire netting
- stub wire or hair pins
- reel wire
- florist's wire
- 2 screw-in hooks for hanging the board
- dry sack moss
- carpet moss
- dried ingredients: larkspur, lavender, eucalyptus, grasses, apple slices (these and other fruits, such as grapefruit, lemon and orange slices, can be purchased ready-freeze-dried), birch stems

Method

• Make a wire netting mould (see p. 24) to cover one side of the board and staple it in place, making sure it is securely attached and that there are no loose or sharp ends.

• Fill the mould with dry sack moss by pushing it through the holes in the netting, packing it firmly but not too tightly.

• Wire up the larkspur, lavender, eucalyptus and grasses into bunches (see p. 26) and, starting at the top of the mould, insert their wires into the moss, creating a 'fan' shape that conceals the board behind. Cover about ⅔ of the mould in this way and then fill the remainder by wiring in the birch stems.

• Make 3 necklaces of apple slices by stringing them onto reel wire, then bind these round the top of the birch stems, pushing the wire ends firmly into the moss behind or tying them to the birch stems themselves to hold them in place.

• Finally, take small pieces of carpet moss and wire them with stub wire or hair pins across the sheaf above the top row of apple slices.

• Mount the sheaf as you would a picture, by stringing a length of strong wire or string between two hooks screwed into the back of the board.

Bunches of dried flowers can, if you're not careful, look insignificant when included in large decorations. When used as the main 'ingredient', however, the effect can be stunning, particularly if they are shaped into a topiary-like tree or ball which will display their colour and individual shapes to the full.

This lavender tree not only looks spectacular; it will also fill a room with scent that will last for weeks. (When it does eventually fade, simply add lavender essence to the pot-pourri.) A wire netting mould is stapled to the top of a birch pole, which is then supported in its glass vase by a mound of lavender pot-pourri. Bunches of lavender are then simply inserted into the mould until it is densely and evenly covered. It's particularly important in instances such as this, where the lavender will not be trimmed to shape, that the initial mould is itself as evenly rounded as possible so that you will not have to compensate for any asymmetrical lumps.

Dried roses are especially attractive, their multi-layered petals contrasting with the simple lines of the decoration as a whole. For the rose ball, short lengths of birch branches were bound and supported by dry sack moss in the urn. A dry oasis ball was then mounted on the top of the birch and covered with rose heads, their stems trimmed to about 2 inches.

A dry oasis also supports the roses in the semicircular dome. This time, however, the mould is set on a birch pole stand (see p. 20). After inserting rose heads into the top of the dome, the cut rose stems are pushed into its underside, splayed to balance the width above. The bottom of the pot is covered with felt to protect the surface on which the decoration will be placed and, as a finishing touch, rich tassled cord 'ties' the display together.
These sprouts, dried and glued to an oasis ball, will be an immediate talking point. The ball itself is glued securely to a narrow cane or stick, around which is bound dried marjoram.

TOPIARY DECORATIONS

It's some time now since I started to make topiary decorations but they remain as popular as ever among my clients, possibly because their unusual yet simple shapes will enhance a host of different settings around the home, and also because, like dried flower decorations, they are long-lasting. They're a particular favourite of mine because of the variety of shapes that can be created.

In my sitting room (see *opposite*), for instance, I have two large moss and cupressus topiary balls mounted on tall stands. Set imposingly in a mirrored alcove opposite the door, their height and shape instantly stop you short as you enter the room.

You're under no obligation, however, to make such large topiary decorations for your own home, although whether the piece be large or small, the methods are identical and very simple. Find an appropriate setting and consider whether one, large decoration would look best, or whether two or three smaller ones clustered together would be more eye-catching. Then think about the shapes: should they be round or rectangular, mushroom-shaped or conical, straight-edged or tiered, or would a combination of shapes look more effective? Compared with fresh or dried flower decorations, where you can shape the materials only to a limited extent, here you have chance to be your most creative and experiment with any number of forms. Remember, too, to choose your container with care. Terracotta pots, with their simple shape and natural colouring, complement most topiary shapes; but you can use any container of your choice as long as its lines don't fight with those of the decoration.

The simple lines and deep green colouring of this **cupressus obelisk** *(p. 62) are seen to most striking effect against an uncluttered, white-washed cottage wall.*

Experimenting with different topiary shapes can produce the most eye-catching decorations. The simple topiary twist around this **candlestand** *(p. 63) turns a humble birch pole support into a table centrepiece that can be used over and over again*

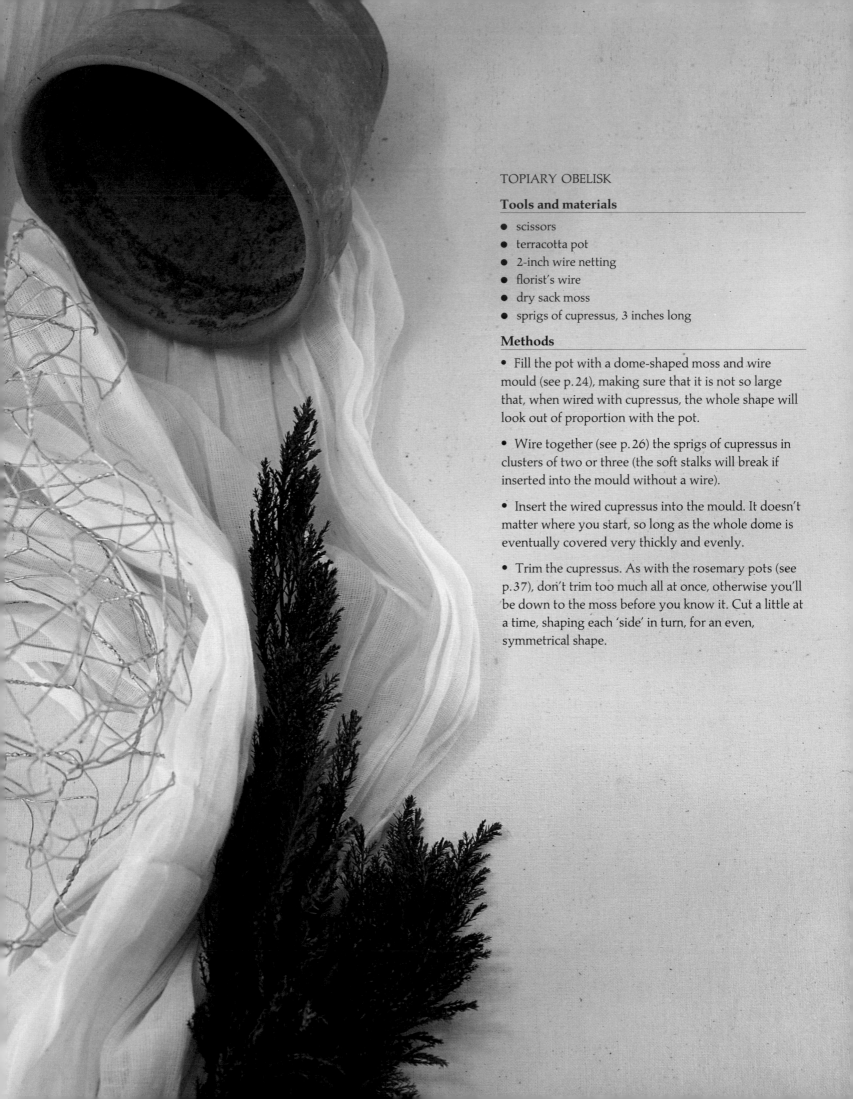

TOPIARY OBELISK

Tools and materials

- scissors
- terracotta pot
- 2-inch wire netting
- florist's wire
- dry sack moss
- sprigs of cupressus, 3 inches long

Methods

• Fill the pot with a dome-shaped moss and wire mould (see p. 24), making sure that it is not so large that, when wired with cupressus, the whole shape will look out of proportion with the pot.

• Wire together (see p. 26) the sprigs of cupressus in clusters of two or three (the soft stalks will break if inserted into the mould without a wire).

• Insert the wired cupressus into the mould. It doesn't matter where you start, so long as the whole dome is eventually covered very thickly and evenly.

• Trim the cupressus. As with the rosemary pots (see p. 37), don't trim too much all at once, otherwise you'll be down to the moss before you know it. Cut a little at a time, shaping each 'side' in turn, for an even, symmetrical shape.

TOPIARY CANDLESTAND

Tools and materials

- scissors
- staple gun
- drill with 1½-inch bit
- terracotta pot large enough to support the pole and candle
- polythene to line pot
- 12-inch birch pole
- finishing plaster or light cement
- 2-inch wire netting
- florist's wire
- dry sack moss
- 12-inch long, 1½-inch diameter candle

Method

- Drill a 1½-inch deep hole in one end of the pole.

- Prepare the birch pole stand (see p. 20).

- Make a moss and wire mould (see p. 24) long enough to snake round the pole.

- Wire the sprigs of cupressus into small bunches (see p. 26).

- Starting at the top of the pole and working round and down to its base, staple the mould in place.

- Insert the wired cupressus into the mould until it is evenly and densely covered.

- Trim the cupressus so that it tapers slightly at the top and base of the pole.

- Set the candle in its hole, securing it with Oasis Fix if necessary.

TERRACOTTA DECORATIONS

Having experimented in familiar surroundings to create decorations from a treasure-trove of natural materials, don't forget the use that can be made of terracotta, whose colour and texture will enhance displays of all kinds.

The terracotta herb and vegetable garden (pp. 18–19), for instance, will bring to life any large kitchen dresser or table. As an alternative, however, you could fill the same display of pots with dried grasses, flowers and pot-pourri and set it on an occasional table in a sitting room or bedroom. Or fill it with small shells, pebbles, pieces of driftwood, and set candles in four or five of the pots for a striking dinner party centrepiece. Or present it and numerous packets of seeds to a young child and let them discover the delights of tending their own, small garden. The possibilities are endless . . .

Terracotta can be used to create much larger decorations, too. The mirror frames pictured below, for instance, fill the walls of a client's sitting room but are no less full of natural, rustic charm for all their size. By painting all the many constituent parts — watering cans, brooms, baskets, spades, rakes, hoes and shears — the same mellow shade, the shapes of each are accentuated rather than diminished, and what could be more appropriate than to give a natural colour to those implements normally used to tend our gardens?

A **terracotta figure** *(pp. 66–7) standing in the corner of a room adds a truly quirky note that will delight children and adults alike. They can be made in almost any size — I have one no more than 10 inches tall on a table at home; this one stands about 24 inches tall, and the pair at the entrance to my shop are life-size. One would also make an ideal present for the floral decorator who thinks he or she has everything . . . if you can bear to part with it.*

TERRACOTTA POT FIGURE

Tools and materials

- scissors
- drill
- glue gun
- 2 very small terracotta pots (for the wrists)
- 16–20 small terracotta pots (legs and arms)
- 1 medium-sized terracotta pot (head)
- 2 large terracotta pots (body)
- polythene to line pots
- finishing plaster or light cement
- light galvanized wire
- bamboo canes or strong sticks
- carpet moss
- dried rosemary (optional)
- dried roses (optional)

Method

• Begin with the feet. Take two of the small pots, line them with polythene and fill with finishing plaster or light cement as if you were making a birch pole support (see p. 20). This time, though, insert a bamboo cane or stick not into the top of the pot, but through the drainage hole in its base. Leave to harden.

• Once the plaster or cement has set and the sticks are firmly held, stand the feet with sticks pointing upwards and place four or five more small pots on top of each, supported by the stick through their drainage holes. Since the pots won't necessarily be uniform, they may not stack evenly. It doesn't matter how many you use, so long as the legs are the same length. Trim the sticks so that they stand above the top of the legs by about 2 inches.

• Take a large pot and drill two holes opposite each other in the pot side at the base. Don't worry if the holes seem to be too large — they can easily be filled with carpet moss. Then stand the legs together and set the large pot on top, making sure the tops of the leg sticks pass through the holes in the pot base.

• Line this pot with polythene, add mixed finishing plaster or light cement and insert another bamboo cane or stick into the centre, as if you were making a birch pole stand (see p. 20). Leave to harden.

• Complete the body by setting the second large pot, inverted, on top of the first so that the bamboo cane or stick passes through its drainage hole and stands proud by a good 6 inches.

• Make the support for the arms by looping a length of galvanized wire around the bamboo near the base of the inverted pot, letting the wire hang down at either side of the 'body', and trimming the ends if necessary so that the 'arms' are the same length.

• Working on one arm at a time, take two or three small pots – again, the number will depend on how evenly the pots will stack – and feed them, base first, up the wire to the top of the body. Once two or three have been wired on, fill around their edges with carpet

moss to hold them together.

• Then make the 'elbow' by wiring on another small pot but setting it at an angle inside the pot above so that it 'bends' towards the body. Add a final, very small pot, wind the remaining wire into a knot at its base and fill any gaps between the pots with carpet moss. Build up the second arm in exactly the same way, making sure it is the same length as the first.

• Take the medium-sized pot and stand it on top of the body, with the remains of the bamboo passing through its drainage hole. To support it and make the 'neck' and 'shoulders', glue carpet moss around the bamboo and galvanized wire and across the pot bases at the tops of the body and arms.

• Conceal the holes at the top of the legs with carpet moss and, as a final flourish, fill the top pot with dried lavender followed by roses all the way round the pot edge.

FLORAL FEASTS

ENTERTAINING AT HOME

Now that you have seen how straightforward are the basic techniques used in floral decoration, and have experimented with ideas of your own, you should feel sufficiently confident to display your decorations in public. Dinner parties provide the ideal opportunity because you can control the scale of the event and provide decorations to suit. You will also almost certainly be surrounded by friends who, while sometimes the harshest of critics, will at least never have the gall to describe your decorations as 'nice'.

In just the same way as a decoration should suit its surroundings around the home, so a dinner-party display should reflect the atmosphere of the occasion, which could be intimate, formal or informal. Each set of decorations will be specific to its environment and sense of occasion, but whatever you create, it should be such that your guests will barely notice whether they are served with chips or caviar.

A SPRING DINNER PARTY

This was held in my conservatory, which now resembles a small jungle. Plants that not so long ago barely stood above their pots now reach up the walls and across the roof; deep green foliage frames the mirrors and windows; the atmosphere is one of idyllic peacefulness.

Into this haven I decided to bring a riot of spring colour. It was mid-February and I wanted to prove that winter was nearly over and spring was on its way. How better to do this than to contrast the dark with the bright and set a bustling array of pots and fresh flowers against the serene deep greens and browns?

I normally have a simple wooden table in the centre of the room but decided that on this occasion a slate-topped table would be more appropriate, contrasting as it would with the vibrant colours of the centrepiece, candlestands and plates. As ever, candles and natural candlestands were a must, with the flames reflected in the mirrors two- and three-fold for a truly magical effect.

Surrounded by dark green foliage, these candlestands, urn and moss-covered pots act as an essential foil to the dazzling main table display.

*At the back stand tall **vine candlestands** (p. 74), the sculptured shape and mottled olive-green shades of their leaves contrasting with the wild, trailing ivy cascading out of the urn in front. To either side are shorter, wrought iron candelabras set on what appear to be moss mounds. These are nothing more than upturned buckets with carpet moss glued on all over and fronds of ivy wrapped around the top for added texture and shape. Lurking underneath the foliage, terracotta nightlights pick out the detail of the urn and moss and complement the small flickering flames dotted around the main table.*

***Terracotta pot candlestands** (p. 75) add natural colour and texture to this spring table display, their height complementing that of the narcissi and hyacinths in the centrepiece (p. 72).*

SPRING DINNER PARTY CENTREPIECE

Tools and materials

- 12 inch diameter terracotta pot
- 18-inch diameter shallow terracotta bowl
- 12 medium-sized terracotta pots
- 20 small terracotta pots
- house plant compost
- damp sack moss
- 12 flowering narcissi
- 10 polyanthus
- 12 flowering hyacinths
- 20 scillas

Method

• Stand the 12-inch pot in the centre of the shallow bowl and fill both with compost to within half-an-inch of their rims. Plant the narcissi in the taller pot and the polyanthus in the bowl, then conceal any soil with sack moss.

• Set the hyacinths individually in the medium-sized pots, the scillas in the small ones, and again cover the top of the compost with sack moss so that the plants look as if they're nestling in their natural habitat.

• Place the large display in the centre of the table and arrange the hyacinths and scillas around it in a wild profusion of spring colours.

VINE-LEAF CANDLESTAND

Tools and materials (for one candlestand)

- scissors
- drill with 1½-inch bit
- terracotta pot large enough to support the pole and candle
- polythene to line the pot
- finishing plaster or light cement
- 18-inch birch pole
- reel wire
- dry sack moss
- vine leaves to cover pole
- 12-inch long, 1½-inch diameter candle

Method

• Drill a 1½-inch deep hole in one end of the birch pole.

• Prepare the birch pole stand (see p. 20).

• Bind the reel wire firmly round the top of the pole. Take four or five vine leaves, hold them, pointing upwards, round the top of the pole and bind them with wire to secure them in place.

• Work your way round and down the pole, binding in more vine leaves. Make sure they overlap evenly to hide the reel wire and give a clean, sculptured look. When you reach the base of the pole, wrap the wire round tightly two or three times and tie it off.

• Fill in around the top of the pot with moss, covering all the plaster or cement and any reel wire that might be visible. Finally, insert the candle, making sure that it is straight – there's absolutely nothing worse, or more unsafe, than a crooked candle!

TERRACOTTA POT CANDLESTAND

Tools and materials (for one candlestand)

- terracotta pot large enough to support the smaller pots and candle
- 7 small terracotta pots
- sack moss
- 12-inch long, 1½-inch diameter candle

Method

• Fill two-thirds of the large terracotta pot with sack moss and set one of the small pots in the centre, packing more moss around it so that it sits securely.

• Place the remaining six small pots one inside the other, turning them to make sure they stand as straight as possible and filling in around the rims with moss if necessary to make them stand without wobbling.

• Fill the top pot with sack moss and insert the candle, adding more moss so that the candle is supported firmly and, as ever, stands straight.

DECORATING PLATES

When decorating plates you really can let your imagination run wild. No tools are required, just a creative eye. More than anything else, these plate decorations reflect an important but often forgotten point about floral decorations: any display should be made for the enjoyment not just of its creator but also of the beholder.

Set alone against the dark slate table, this warm, daffodil-yellow under-plate would have looked too severe, but with its line broken by spring flowers, the effect is devastating. I used heads, petals and sprigs of tulips, jasmine, japonica, polyanthus, trusty rosemary, ivy and feverfew grouped in gay abandon, their colours reflecting those of the top plate.

Thus inspired, you can make plate decorations a theme for several dinner parties, each time varying the colours and style to complement the occasion. This vivid setting conjures up nothing so much as a late, relaxed supper at the tail end of some hot Mediterranean day when the air is *still warm and full of scent.*

Reflecting my love of bright, clashing colours, I chose petals, small flowers and leaves in vibrant oranges, pinks, reds and greens, boldly set off against the deep blue cloth. Since the petals and flowers are arranged between the *under-plate and the top plate, it may be advisable to use a third plate for serving so that the decoration is held in position.*

Perhaps the occasion is a grand one, requiring a more formal approach.

Undecorated, this large, gold under-plate may well have looked too heavy in comparison with the exquisite, patterning of the top plate. However, broken up as it is with foliage, it only enhances the overall design. To reflect the delicate colours of the top plate, I used as many subtle shades of green as I could find, with small pieces of mint, ivy, eucalyptus, hellebore, fennel, rue, as well as soft buds of pussy willow.

Outrageous? Not if you imagine a barbecue on the beach after a long day in the sun. Tired and warm, you may be looking forward to a leisurely meal and, even if it is to consist of nothing more than bread, cheese and fruit, it can be set off to advantage with natural decorations that reflect your surroundings and are simple and, above all, fun to create. If starfish are not easy to come by, just place some small pebbles or intriguingly shaped fragments of driftwood around the plate for a truly spontaneous display.

SHELL AND BAMBOO CENTREPIECES

I know I have said a great deal about my love of vivid colours, but it is nature as a whole that inspires me, and my imagination is therefore as fired by its serene and subtle lines and shades as it is by its more exuberant hues. For it's only by appreciating both that one realizes that nature's beauty is inherently and inextricably balanced.

When selecting materials and creating designs in the simplest of styles, I have found particular inspiration over the years from trips to the Far East, especially Japan. It's not just that the natural landscapes are like nothing else I've ever seen; it's that the 'cultivated' landscapes reflect nature's simplicity to perfection. A Japanese rock garden, for instance, with its use of rocks, pebbles, water and judiciously placed trees and flowers, creates the most peaceful of havens.

At home, I try to incorporate some of the ideas I have seen on my travels into my designs. When finished, the decorations won't be exact copies of displays I've seen elsewhere; they will capture some of the ideas, but also reflect my own style — this is what I mean by saying you should let your imagination be inspired to the extent that you create your own style. And, as ever, I wait for the right moment to display these new ideas to what I hope will be the best effect, looking above all at the setting to see whether it's appropriate — there's absolutely no point in spending hours making a subtle pebble and bound bamboo decoration for a room full of Victorian clutter: the effect would be totally lost.

If I have a particular idea that I want to try out, and I can't wait for the right situation to present itself, then I simply make it happen, and I suggest you do the same. When you're asked to prepare displays for a particular occasion and are given *carte blanche* to do whatever you like — or even, being more realistic, if you want to transform a corner of your own home for no other reason than that the mood takes you — think of all those ideas for decorations you've had that you've never had the opportunity to experiment with. Think of what you will need by way of accessories — a particular table, screen, urn, statue, basket, for instance — find, beg or borrow it and set to work.

This is exactly what I did with these shell and bamboo candlestands (*right*). I had had in mind ideas for simple, chic decorations using more unusual and Oriental materials for so long that if I hadn't tried them out, they'd have gone stale for waiting. I borrowed the screen, the tablecloth, the plates, the glasses . . . and as soon as I had them, everything fell into place.

The screen, in its simplicity, acts as the most dramatic of backdrops for the whole display, yet it does not intrude. The glasses mirror the natural, straight lines of the bamboo and also the fluted cut of the shells; the subdued shades of cloth, serviettes and plates set off the natural tones of the decorations without overpowering them. As a restful corner in a room otherwise full of people and chatter, it works to perfection.

SHELL AND BAMBOO CENTREPIECE

Tools and materials

- scissors
- glue gun
- drill with $\frac{1}{8}$-inch bit
- large plastic bowl
- 3×12-inch, $\frac{1}{2}$ inch diamater candle
- 3×12-inch pieces of bamboo wide enough to hold the candles
- finishing plaster or light cement
- florist's wire
- piece of light straw matting to cover the base and lower edge of the bowl
- about 20 large scallop shells
- carpet moss
- lichen moss
- small stones or pebbles
- fresh rushes
- rough string

Method

• Glue the matting to the base and lower edge of the bowl.

• Cover the rest of the outside of the bowl with shells. Take the shells one at a time and, starting at the top of the bowl, hold each shell against the plastic so that its widest edge stands slightly proud of the bowl rim. Drill two holes about an inch apart through both the base of the shell and the bowl. Still holding the shell in place, wire it to the bowl with florist's wire, twisting the wire ends together and pressing them flat on the inside.

• Attach shells in this way in an even row all round the bowl rim, overlapping their edges a little so that they look like the petals of a flower, and then start on the second row.

• Arrange each shell in this row so that it overlaps

with one in the row above and, holding it firmly in place, drill two holes through the new shell. Drill right through the plastic, as before, then wire securely in place.

• Continue until the bowl is covered and all that's visible are small sections of the straw matting round the bottom edge.

• Cover the small sections of wire visible on the outside of the shells by gluing on small pieces of lichen moss.

• Fill the bowl with finishing plaster or light cement, as if you were preparing a birch pole support (see p. 20), and insert the bamboo poles. Once the plaster or cement has hardened, cover it with carpet moss.

• Cut 3-inch lengths off the bottom ends of the rushes and put to one side. Gather the longer pieces into bundles and arrange them on top of the moss, criss-crossing them between the bamboo poles.

• Take the remaining, short pieces and bind them together in groups of 10–12 with lengths of rough string. Then simply arrange these on top of the rush pile.

• Set the pebbles in any gaps round the edge of the bowl and then insert the candles in the tops of the bamboo, securing them with glue or Oasis Fix. The joints in the bamboo will dictate how deep the candles sink until they reach their support, and give a multi-levelled, utterly natural look.

SHELL PETAL CANDLESTAND

Tools and materials (for one candlestand)

- scissors
- glue gun
- terracotta pot large enough to support the bamboo pole and candle
- polythene to line pot
- finishing plaster or light cement
- 3 × 18-inch lengths of narrow bamboo
- carpet moss
- lichen moss
- 6 scallop shells
- rough string
- 5-inch long, 2½-inch diameter candle

Method

• Prepare the bamboo support as you would a birch pole stand (see p.20), holding the three lengths of bamboo firmly together when you insert them in the plaster or cement.

• Starting at the top of the bamboo, glue 3–4 shells around the poles so that they fan out at about 45°. Glue a second layer of shells under the first, but fan them out horizontally, making sure they fill the spaces left by the first layer. Seen from above, they should look like an opening flower. Leave to dry.

• Glue lichen moss around and between the shell bases to fill any gaps and conceal all the glue.

• With lengths of string, bind the poles together in a couple of places and surround their base with carpet moss to cover the plaster or cement.

• Lastly, sit the candle on its shell base and glue firmly in position.

A FIRESIDE SUPPER

I've rearranged the layout of the furniture in all my rooms at home so many times that even regular visitors have lost track. I love being able to change things to create a specific mood and am especially fond of having several different areas in which to entertain, be it in the window, framed by large palms overlooking the garden, or round a low table and sofa or, as in this case, with a welcoming fire as the centrepiece.

There's no reason why you can't do the same. Changing the position of even one piece of furniture may encourage you to make a completely clean sweep and it's extraordinary how a room that has become 'set in its ways' suddenly takes on a new lease of life with a bit of furniture removal. This will also open up areas for which to create a new decoration.

On this occasion (see *right*), I pulled the table that had been sitting in the window into the centre of the room towards the

hearth and set a large palm behind it to break the now empty bay. Bearing in mind that I wanted to create as warm an atmosphere as possible, I looked for vibrant reds and pinks for the tablecloths and place settings. To complement the colours in these, I hauled over a bust and plinth from the far end of the room and set them by the fire, balancing those opposite. I then draped them both in **garlands of deep green foliage** (p.95) for a rich but cooling contrast with the main table. In the meantime, Bumble, one of my two dogs, settled herself down in front of the flames, right in my way, oblivious to any notions of artistic balance.

For the table decorations themselves, I planned to mirror both the warming fire and the refreshingly cool greens of the garlands. In the centre, I set a rich bowl of red and pink tulips together with guelder foliage for contrast in colour and shape. These were simply set in a wire mould in a large bowl of water, the bowl covered in carpet moss. Around this I placed four **wax-flower candlestands** (p.94). These hardy little flowers are ideal for fresh decorations as they are particularly long-lasting and the delicate shape combined with the deep pink shade of this particular variety were ideal for the setting. Neither the garland, the central bowl nor the candlestands took long to make once I had planned the whole effect and this is something that ought to be true of any display. Once you have done all the planning, the actual execution of the decorations should be done carefully but does not necessarily take the lion's share of the time; it's the planning and preparation that can be time-consuming.

The room was now rearranged to my (and the dogs') liking. As soon as it was done, however, I immediately started to plan the next 'removal' (the dogs won't mind as long as I don't block their way to the hearth).

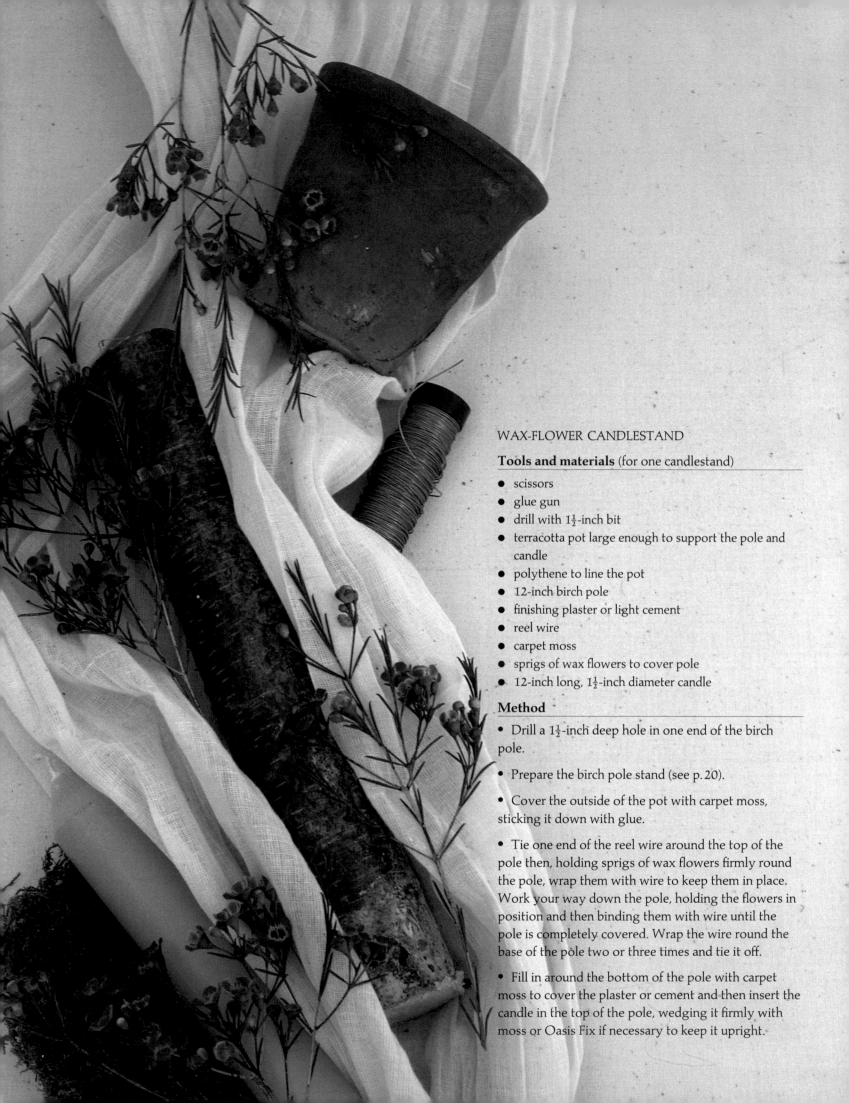

WAX-FLOWER CANDLESTAND

Tools and materials (for one candlestand)

- scissors
- glue gun
- drill with 1½-inch bit
- terracotta pot large enough to support the pole and candle
- polythene to line the pot
- 12-inch birch pole
- finishing plaster or light cement
- reel wire
- carpet moss
- sprigs of wax flowers to cover pole
- 12-inch long, 1½-inch diameter candle

Method

- Drill a 1½-inch deep hole in one end of the birch pole.

- Prepare the birch pole stand (see p. 20).

- Cover the outside of the pot with carpet moss, sticking it down with glue.

- Tie one end of the reel wire around the top of the pole then, holding sprigs of wax flowers firmly round the pole, wrap them with wire to keep them in place. Work your way down the pole, holding the flowers in position and then binding them with wire until the pole is completely covered. Wrap the wire round the base of the pole two or three times and tie it off.

- Fill in around the bottom of the pole with carpet moss to cover the plaster or cement and then insert the candle in the top of the pole, wedging it firmly with moss or Oasis Fix if necessary to keep it upright.

FOLIAGE GARLAND

Tools and materials

- scissors
- 2-inch wire netting
- stub wire or hair pins
- damp sack moss
- polythene sheeting to back garland
- foliage – I used rosemary, eucalyptus, ivy, catkins, winter sweet, lauristinus, camellia and silver leaf, but you can include whatever is readily available.

Method

• Prepare a moss and wire garland mould as described on p. 24.

• Take a look at all the foliage with a view to the different leaf shapes, colours and textures. Which ones will act as a strong, vibrant background? Which are the more delicate ones that will be better displayed at the front? Sort the foliage out into two or three piles according to their shape, size and colour.

• Beginning with the background foliage, insert the branches and stems into the garland, working your way from top to bottom until the area is evenly covered with a wild profusion of naturally hanging foliage with plenty of movement. Continue with the second pile in the same way and finish with the more delicate leaves.

• Pin the protective polythene to the back of the garland (see p. 24) and then simply drape it above the fireplace or over furniture, or hang it up in all its glory.

YELLOW ROSE GARLAND

Tools and materials

- scissors
- reel wire
- florist's wire
- carpet moss
- about 25 bunches of small roses

Method

• This is one of the simplest of garlands to make, yet can be twisted to stunning effect to snake down a long table.

• Take about 10 or 12 roses depending on their size, trim the stalks to around 5 inches and wire together (see p. 26).

• Wire all the roses into small bunches in this way. Then, placing the heads of one bunch against the stalks of another, bind together with reel wire. If there seems to be a lot of stalk showing, simply cover it by wiring in small pieces of carpet moss as you go.

• Wire together all the bunches of roses like this, tying in carpet moss if necessary, until you have a long, sinuous garland. There's no need to tie off the reel wire as soon as you've joined two bunches — if they're attached firmly enough, the wire will hold until you have the next bunch ready.

As a variation, you might like to use roses in two complementary shades and/or sizes (see the **carpet moss and fresh rose garland**, pp. 30–1).

YELLOW ROSE CANDLESTAND

Tools and materials (for one candlestand)

- scissors
- drill with 1½-inch bit
- terracotta pot large enough to support the pole and candle
- polythene to line the pot
- finishing plaster or light cement
- 18-inch birch pole
- reel wire
- carpet moss
- 40–50 bunches of small yellow roses
- 12-inch long, 1½-inch diameter candle

Method

• Drill a 1½-inch deep hole in one end of the birch pole.

• Prepare the birch pole stand (see p. 20).

• Trim the stalks of the roses to about 3 inches.

• Attach the reel wire to the top of the pole. Take a small bunch of roses and, holding them so that they are evenly spaced around the pole, with heads pointing upwards, bind them securely in place with wire.

• Work your way round and down the pole, binding the bunches so that their heads overlap with the stalks of those above to hide the reel wire. When you reach the base, firmly wrap the wire round three or four times and tie it off.

• Fill in around the top of the pot with carpet moss to hide the plaster or cement and then insert the candle in the top of the pole, securing it with moss or Oasis Fix to keep it steady and straight.

For contrast with the brilliant yellow of the top table, yet to complement the rich decor, I filled the centres of the many smaller tables with a variety of fresh flower and box candlestands. The whole room was walled with mirrors and once all of the 600 or so candles were lit, the effect as the flames at all heights were reflected four-fold was as breathtaking as I had hoped it would be.

The bowls in the centre of each table were simply filled with a wire mould and water (see p. 24) for displays of spring flowers in vibrant pinks, purples, yellows and greens, but to add width and movement to the raised bowls, I added cascading fronds of forsythia.

The box candlestands were prepared in just the same way as I would any wired pole decoration – a good example of what I mean when I say there's no need to change the way you work just because you have more than one display to make. Just ensure you have all the materials you need and allow yourself plenty of time.

The small box candlestands follow the method for the **yellow rose stand** (see p. 101). The longer poles, however, were too tall to stand safely in pots on their own. Instead, they were screwed securely to a circular board, with the bowls of flowers set in the middle. The very tall poles were also joined about halfway up with another board on which, again, was set a floral display.

LEMON WREATH

Tools and materials

- scissors
- 2-inch wire netting – if the wreath is to be set around another centrepiece decoration, make sure the wire is long enough to reach all the way round with a good 8 inches to spare
- stub wire
- florist's wire
- dry sack moss
- lemons
- polythene to line the bottom of the finished wreath

Method

• Prepare a moss and wire garland mould (see p. 24). Instead of being flat, however, this one is round; it should also be particularly firm so that it supports the weight of the lemons. Once finished, bind the two ends together with florist's wire.

• Wire up the lemons one at a time (see p. 26).

• Starting round the bottom outside edge of the wreath, wire in the lemons one after another, leaving no gaps in the mould.

• Wire in a second row above the first so that the lemons nestle between those below. Continue until the whole of the wreath's outer side is covered.

• Finally, pin the protective polythene to the wreath base (see p. 24).

A BOWL OF POLYANTHUS

Tools and materials

- scissors
- glue gun
- large plastic bowl
- carpet moss to cover bowl
- house plant compost
- polyanthus — I used yellow and purple for this centrepiece to complement the colours of the tablecloths, but polyanthus come in such a variety of vibrant shades that a mixture also makes a glorious display.

Method

• Turn the bowl upside down and cover all but the base with carpet moss, sticking it down with glue.

• Set the bowl the right way up and fill it with house plant compost. If the polyanthus are already in their own soil, don't shake it off; simply use a little extra compost to fill the gaps once the plants are arranged.

• Look at the colours of the polyanthus, and plant them in the bowl to create the most vibrant yet natural effect — no straight lines of flowers of the same colour, but pinks next to clashing orange, for instance, or variegated next to deep red for contrast.

• Once the bowl is full, fill in around the edge with carpet moss to hide any compost and set it in the centre of the table, either on its own or surrounded by the wreath of lemons, opposite.

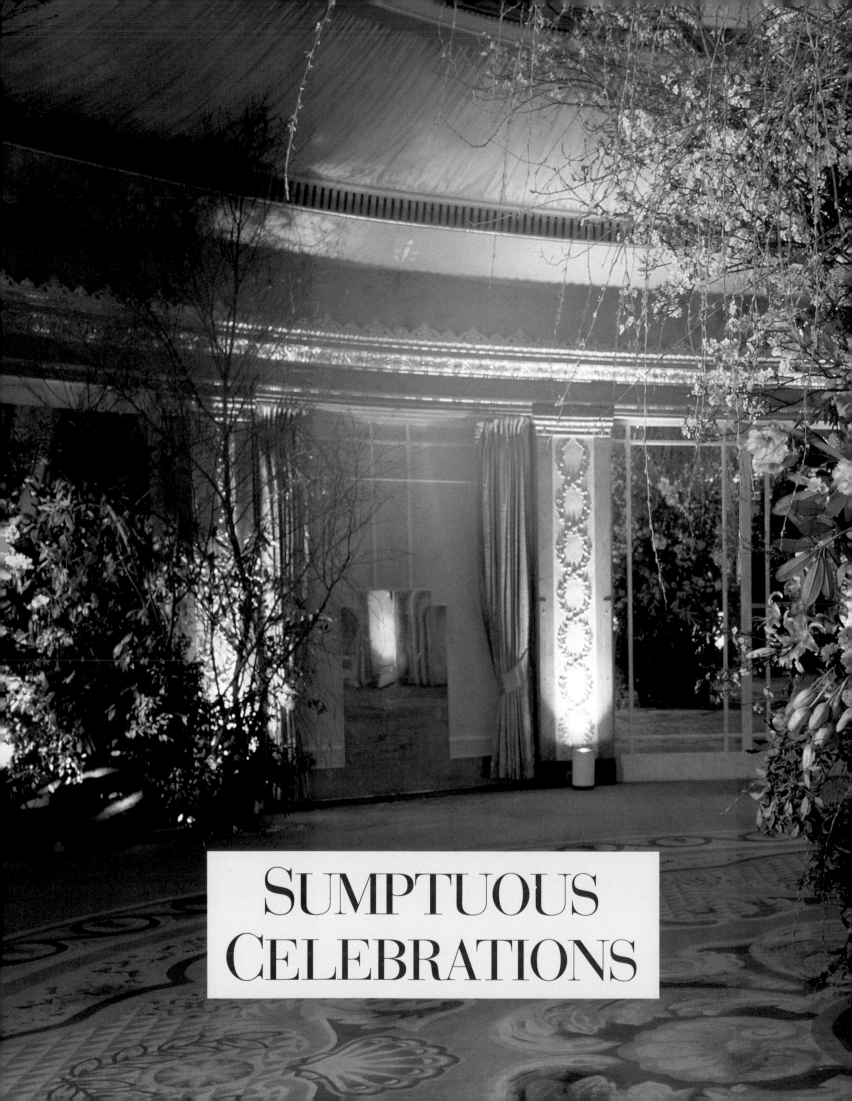

SUMPTUOUS
CELEBRATIONS

PLANNING AND PREPARATION

There's nothing like a celebration, be it an anniversary party, wedding, Christmas or Thanksgiving, to allow you to create your most exuberant of decorations and to display your skills to the full. Simply remember to take into account first, the setting; and second, the season or date of the event, and allow yourself plenty of time for the planning and preparation.

SETTING

This could be a castle or chapel, a hotel or village hall, but whatever it is, pay a couple of visits at least, particularly if it is unfamiliar to you. Take notes when you go and draw sketches of features or areas you consider might be appropriate for displays.

There may be times when a visit in advance is impossible: a marquee, for example, might not go up until very shortly before the event. In this case, you'll need answers to questions such as what are the maximum and minimum heights? How wide is the entrance? What will it contain in the way of furniture? Will the floor be solid boards or grass? The answers will dictate the scale of your decorations; whether, for example, you can make bouquets for the backs of chairs or ends of benches, or whether long floor garlands would be more appropriate; and whether displays will stand alone safely or need support.

SEASON

The more warning you are given of a celebration the better, but don't forget to look ahead when choosing the materials you are going to use. If the event is to take place in mid-summer, and you are approached in early spring, make a list of the flowers that will be in full bloom in June and July, not late February and March. Likewise, if you are planning in May for an event in September, think of the richness of autumn fruits and berries because bluebells, for example, are going to be hard to find, and wholly inappropriate if you do lay your hands on any.

Nothing more nor less than these simple considerations helped to shape the celebratory decorations (*right*).

In the anterooms adjoining the ballroom of the Dorchester Hotel in London I created a woodland grove for a spring wedding reception. As the guests arrived, they first wandered through a mirrored hall with a pillared alcove (*right*). Deep green foliage, 'planted' in carpet moss all around, complemented the rich colours and twisting shapes of the mural and, being reflected in all directions, created a magical, fairytale atmosphere.

From here, the guests entered the main 'glade' (*see previous pages*), an oval room in exquisite pastel shades with a painted, domed ceiling, one central pillar – a trellised bird cage – and recesses each containing a spotlit statue (*overleaf*).

Binding a wire netting frame to the central pillar, I inserted cascading spring blossom, forsythia, rhododendron foliage, weeping willow, prunus, guelder, French tulips, amaryllis, lilies and azaleas, planting flowers in extenders full of water not just to keep them fresh but also to give the display greater width and movement.

The alcoves and statues were just asking to be decorated with a profusion of foliage – willow, ilex, rhododendron – against which nestled brightly coloured spring flowers such as narcissi and polyanthus.

Preparing decorations such as these is the most exhilarating of experiences. No amount of practice at a floral decorator's techniques can prepare you for it: all you need is the thoughtful preparation described and you really can let your imagination take over.

A FORMAL CELEBRATION

Compared with the springtime wedding, the launch of an autumn exhibition at the Royal Academy — a celebration, certainly, but one of greater formality — demanded much more 'self-controlled' if no less magnificent decorations.

The main feature of the entrance hall is the imposing staircase that leads up to the exhibition rooms themselves. With tall marble pillars on either side and at both ends, and with two half-landings making for a leisurely ascent, the staircase simply had to be the focal point for the decorations.

To complement the pillars' grandeur without swamping it, I decked them in long garlands. Into the usual damp sack moss and wire mould I wired in large-headed fresh flowers such as hydrangeas, bunches of roses, as well as rosemary, cotoneaster, ornamental cabbages and gourds, to create large splashes of colour in proportion to the scale of the setting.

When making a garland of this size — the longest ones measured over 40 feet — the best thing to do is to make it in short sections which can be transported more easily and wire these together just before you hang them. The most important thing is to ensure that there are people on hand to help you set up, whatever kind of large decoration you're preparing. It took three of us up one long ladder, with a fourth holding the base, plus one up a shorter, supporting ladder, to bind the longest of these garlands to the tallest pillar with strong rope.

On the half-landings and at the top of the stairs, I set 6-foot birch pole candlestands. The pole was cemented firmly into a large pot in the normal way, but two-thirds of the way up each, I drilled and screwed in three or four shorter poles (depending whether the stand was to be placed flat against a wall or had space on all sides). Onto the ends of all the poles were attached small pots for the candles, secured with a screw through their drainage hole.

The poles were wrapped in damp sack moss and netting, into which first was wired bunch after bunch of rosemary. The scent these gave off throughout the evening gave a final flourish to the whole display. On top of and around the rosemary were bunches of roses, hydrangeas and cotoneaster, whose colours complemented not just the garland but also the subtle shades of the marble decor.

On this occasion, the candles, for safety reasons, were artificial, supported in their pots by moss — but they were still straight!

WEDDINGS

15-foot decorated trellises and the 40-foot garlands are relatively rare, if exciting, events. You're much more likely to be expected or asked to provide the decorations for a wedding, be it for a member of the family or for a friend. Bridal flowers deserve a section of their own (see pp. 127–37), but planning the displays for the venue where the ceremony is to be held follows exactly the procedures I have just described. Look at the setting and take account of the season. Also, and this is true of all occasions but particularly of weddings, find out whether the host or bride has particular preferences or ideas for the types of display and where they should be placed. You may well find that the organizers of a large function have approached you precisely because they have no notion of where to begin and know you will be able to create just the right decorations without any further guidance. Since weddings are always such personal occasions, however, the bride, her mother — or both — will almost certainly have suggestions to make (which may not necessarily be the same — diplomacy is another prerequisite when preparing for such celebrations).

However many opinions you have to take into account, the decorations should, as always, complement not just the surroundings but also each other for the greatest impact. Weddings, moreover, give you the scope to make both large and small displays for the same event, as in addition to the magnificent decorations at the entrance to the church or reception or altar, there will nearly always be a dark but significant corner in which to place a candlestand, or chair backs or pew ends that could be brightened with bouquets.

LARGE DISPLAYS

These can be free-standing or attached to

a pillar, doorpost or other structure. In either case, make sure that the decoration is not only sumptuous, but safe.

For a summer wedding in a country church (*opposite*), I simply filled a damp moss and wire support, mounted securely against the door frame, with showers of roses in full bloom, smothering the base in moss and grasses for the most natural effect.

The large spring display (p. 118) was mounted on a free-standing base (p. 20) of birch poles in cement, with a cradle at the top holding the bowl and its flowers and branches in a wire mould. Given its size, however, and the fact that people would be passing in front of it, it had to be made absolutely safe. This was done by binding one of the birch poles to the railings behind.

Cascading fronds of ivy, blackberries and cotoneaster provide the natural outline and plenty of movement in this display of autumnal abundance. The support is a damp moss and wire mould, into which the foliage 'backdrop' was inserted first, followed by lilies, and roses wired together in large bunches in keeping with the overall proportions of the display and its surroundings. For balance and additional colour, shape and texture, wired apples were set in a large cluster towards the base and, nestling around them, artichokes and ornamental cabbages.

A winter wedding in this rich, ornate setting called for the warmest and most vibrant of displays. The free-standing support was first bound with moss and branches to conceal it, Then, into the bowl and wire mould at the top of the support, foliage in wild profusion — ivy, variegated holly, pine, eucalyptus — was inserted, to establish balanced height and width. Thereafter, amaryllis set in tubes or extenders and bunches of wired roses were added, their striking colours contrasting with the foliage and the deep brown of the surrounding wood. Golden lilies and fronds of cotoneaster echoed the decorative giltwork of the altar panelling behind.

FREE-STANDING SPRING DISPLAY

Tools and materials

The support:

- scissors
- saw
- staple gun
- tape measure or ruler
- 2 large watertight containers, one for the base, the other to hold the display
- 3 birch poles – those used here were about 4 feet long, but choose the length that will best fit the display you have in mind, making sure that you have a base container large enough to support them
- 1 × 1-inch length of wood for the cradle
- finishing plaster or light cement
- nails or screws
- strong, waterproof adhesive tape
- piece of green or brown hessian or sacking

The display:

- 2-inch wire netting
- reel wire
- florist's wire
- plastic tubes or extenders
- long, supple branches of, for example, dogwood, laurel and willow to cover the birch poles
- variety of fresh flowers and foliage, such as forsythia, ivy, tulips, daffodils, amaryllis, guelder, lauristinus
- raffia

Method

The support:

- Trim the poles so that they are all about the same length – this support is more functional than a work of art, so concentrate on making is sturdy rather than beautiful. If securely made, it can be used again and again for any number of displays.

- Fill the large container with finishing plaster or light cement and set the poles in the mixture, spacing them evenly around the container's edge. Leave to harden.

- Once the poles are secure, make the cradle for the display bowl. About three-quarters of the way up from the base, measure the distances between the poles and cut three lengths of 1 × 1-inch wood to fit. Screw or nail the pieces to the insides of the poles to form a triangular-shaped support.

- Set the container for the display in the centre of the cradle and then tape it to the poles at its rim to hold it in position.

- Conceal the base of the support in hessian or sacking, stapling the material edges to the birch poles.

The display:

• Take the laurel, willow and dogwood branches and trim them to the height of the support. Bind them with reel or florist's wire to the poles and the cradle all the way round until the spaces are all but filled. Then tie them together with a length of raffia to hold them in position.

• Make a tall, firm, dome-shaped wire netting mould, set it in the display bowl and securely attach it with reel wire to the container and cradle. Fill the container with water.

• Starting with the longest branches of display materials, such as the forsythia and ivy, insert them through the wire mould into the water to give the display its basic shape. Then fill in with groups of the tulips, daffodils, amaryllis, guelder and lauristinus, setting in water-filled tubes or extenders those that will not reach the water in the bowl. Continue until the mould is completely concealed and, more than that, looks as if it could not hold one more daffodil or sprig of forsythia, however small.

Interiors such as this magnificent church with its rich decor yet abundance of natural light, offer a host of possibilities if you simply go in with your eyes and mind open and allow the features to strike you as spontaneously as possible.

The first thing I noticed when I went to plan the displays was the width of the central aisle and the vibrant, warm red of its carpet. I immediately resolved to highlight both its width and length, while breaking its straight edges, and began to plan the garland, which eventually ran from the main entrance right up to the front pews.

Thereafter, the types and size of the displays fell naturally into place. The garland had a beginning and an end, both of which needed highlighting with a decoration of some kind. But that left the centre of the church unadorned, so something was needed to run parallel to the garland, but which would also add height.

At the back of the church, on either side of the aisle, were two imposing, dark marble pillars. To mark this grand entrance – and also herald the start of the garlands, I mounted two enormous displays of moss and wire filled with deep green trailing foliage, hydrangeas, roses, cotoneaster, all bound with a large raffia bow, which added a quirky, rustic note to the otherwise grand setting.

The garland itself, made in sections and bound together once in place, was filled with cotoneaster, rosemary, oak, sedum, blackberries, hydrangeas, ornamental cabbages and ivy – a sea of pinks, reds, purples and greens with plenty of natural texture and movement to contrast with and highlight the carpet.

Following the garland down the aisle, the eye automatically fell on the wide altar with its gilded pillars on either side. Next to each I set a tall candlestand (see *overleaf*) to reflect but also to soften their lines.

Down the sides of the church, on the otherwise bare pillars supporting the balcony, were hung further displays of trailing foliage, roses and autumn fruits and berries, which broke the pillars' severe lines and gave height to the displays as a whole.

Compared with the ebullient displays in the body of the church, the candlestands at the altar were more muted, yet more appropriate for the rich, dark colours of their immediate surroundings.

The support was the usual birch pole stand on top of which was screwed a small terracotta pot holding a candle wedged firmly into a bed of moss. The pole was bound with wire netting, knitted and stapled in place, through which was packed damp sack moss. Salmon pink roses wired in clusters of three, hydrangeas, bunches of blackberries and sedum were then wired into the moss from top to bottom.

This was an autumn wedding and the materials were chosen accordingly, but candlestands such as these are simple, striking decorations for a wedding at any time of the year providing the setting is appropriate.

In spring, fill the moss with, for instance, narcissi, tulips, magnolia or guelder. For a winter wedding, holly leaves and berries, bound cinnamon sticks, red apples, sprigs of fir, gourds or pomegranates would all look superb.

PEW ENDS OR CHAIR BACKS

These provide bright, eye-catching splashes of natural colour and shape to the darkest and most severe of interiors. Their use, however, need not be confined to weddings or other large celebrations. Decorative chair backs are simple to make (p. 125) and can be created to grace any kind of dinner party, when they will be an immediate talking point.

The pew ends illustrated here, however, do add a particularly exuberant tone to the rich but dark setting. The salmon-pink roses look almost luminous against the wood and the fronds of berries and

foliage provide plenty of natural movement to contrast with the peaceful, but static, surroundings.

A celebration of spring in a flurry of bright colours set against a contrasting background of rich green velvet swags. Supple fronds of forsythia give the displays their width, height and movement, the daffodils, hyacinths and tulips add the final, jubilant note.

This autumnal pew end sets a profusion of colours, shapes and textures against not only the rich brown wood of the pews, but also its immaculate white bow. Stocks and tall roses provide the height, while seasonal fruits and berries nestle underneath and, as a focal point above the ribbon, an ornamental cabbage adds a humorous but wholly natural flourish.

PEW ENDS AND DECORATIVE CHAIR BACKS

Tools and materials

- scissors
- reel wire
- florist's wire
- raffia or ribbon
- seasonal flowers, foliage, fruits and berries

Method

• I'd be stating the obvious if I simply said tie everything together in a bunch, but that, more or less, is exactly what you do. The 'bunch', however, should be flat on one side to rest snugly against the pew or chair, so when you arrange the materials, do so on a table or worktop.

• There will be some materials, such as the ornamental cabbage in the ribboned pew end opposite, that will need wiring up (see p.26) before they can be added to the display. Prepare all such items before making a start on the final arrangement.

• Then look at the flowers, foliage, fruits and other ingredients you have assembled with a view to their colours, textures and shapes and lay them out, grouping smaller items and allowing larger ones to display their full width or height.

• Once you're satisfied that you have a balanced, natural display, firmly bind the stalks and wires with reel wire, and then conceal this with a raffia or ribboned bow.

• To hang the display, either attach the ends of a further length of wire to the back of the display to form a large hook that can be looped over the pew end or chair back or, if that will not hold it securely, bind it in position with fine reel wire, which can easily be hidden behind the bow or under the flowers.

THE BRIDE

I never eavesdrop, but I did once witness two ladies deep in a conversation so animated it would have been difficult for anyone within twenty yards to avoid picking up at least the gist of what they were saying. From the arm-waving and business-like yet rather frenetic air of one, it was clear she was the mother of the bride; her friend the stoical support.

'And how's the dress coming along?' asked the friend.

'Oh, it's going to be absolutely out of this world . . . I mean, she could get away with wearing practically anything, of course, given her figure, but I really do think the designer has got it just right. So simple. Such classic lines. So flattering. We had a little trouble with the colour, but I'm sure I was right – ivory is so subtle, don't you think?'

'Yes, absolutely . . .'

'And then there are the shoes. Exquisite. Just *made* for the dress. They'll have to be dyed, of course, and I do wonder whether they could do with a bit of embroidered detail – just a little decoration. What d'you think?'

'Without seeing them, or the dress, it's a bit difficult to tell. But it sounds as if you don't want anything too fussy if the dress is so chic. And you'll have to be careful when you choose the flowers. Are the bouquet and headdress organized?'

'Oh, that's all arranged. The flowers'll be very nice . . .'

There's that word again. All that preparation, down to the last bead and bobble on the shoes, and flowers that are *nice*. A bouquet and hair piece can make or ruin the overall effect if they don't complement the bride and style of her dress and their planning and design should be given as much time and care as everything else. They are not difficult to make and there are only a few simple tips to bear in mind:

● as with any detailed display, allow yourself plenty of time to plan and prepare, buying fresh, closed flowers at least 24 hours before the event so that they'll be open and looking their best when the times comes. Try to make the bouquet or hair piece as close as you can to the time it is needed. If they have to be kept for a few hours, place them in a cool room, spray them and then cover them with tissue paper.

● you won't need a great deal in the way of equipment, but do have ready a pair of sharp scissors and the finest reel and florist's wire you can find, as well as rolls of Guttacoll, or stemwind, in green for bouquets, brown and cream for hair pieces.

● hair pieces should be made by binding the flowers to wire which can be pinned securely to fit the bride's hair style, rather than combs which are less flexible and will often slip. Wire hair pieces, unlike combs, can also be trimmed to fit.

● always snip pollen out of the centre of flowers if there is any chance that it might drop and stain the dress – lilies, for instance, are notorious – and always bind the stem ends with raffia, likewise to prevent staining.

Full but beautifully simple dresses can be complemented by large bouquets of fresh flowers and trailing dark green foliage. OPPOSITE, lilies, roses, double tulips, jasmine and ranunculus in white and shades of cream are set against rich green ivy; the **hair piece** *(p. 129) echoes the colours and abundance of the bouquet, with ranunculus, lilies, rosemary, feverfew and guelder. BELOW, a simple yet stunning crown of variegated ivy is easily made by twisting fronds together, securing them with wire. It, too, will complement its* **bouquet** *(p. 128), with its trailing fronds and clusters of ranunculus, guelder, roses, elaeagnus, magnolia leaves, lilacs, lily of the valley, azaleas and rosemary.*

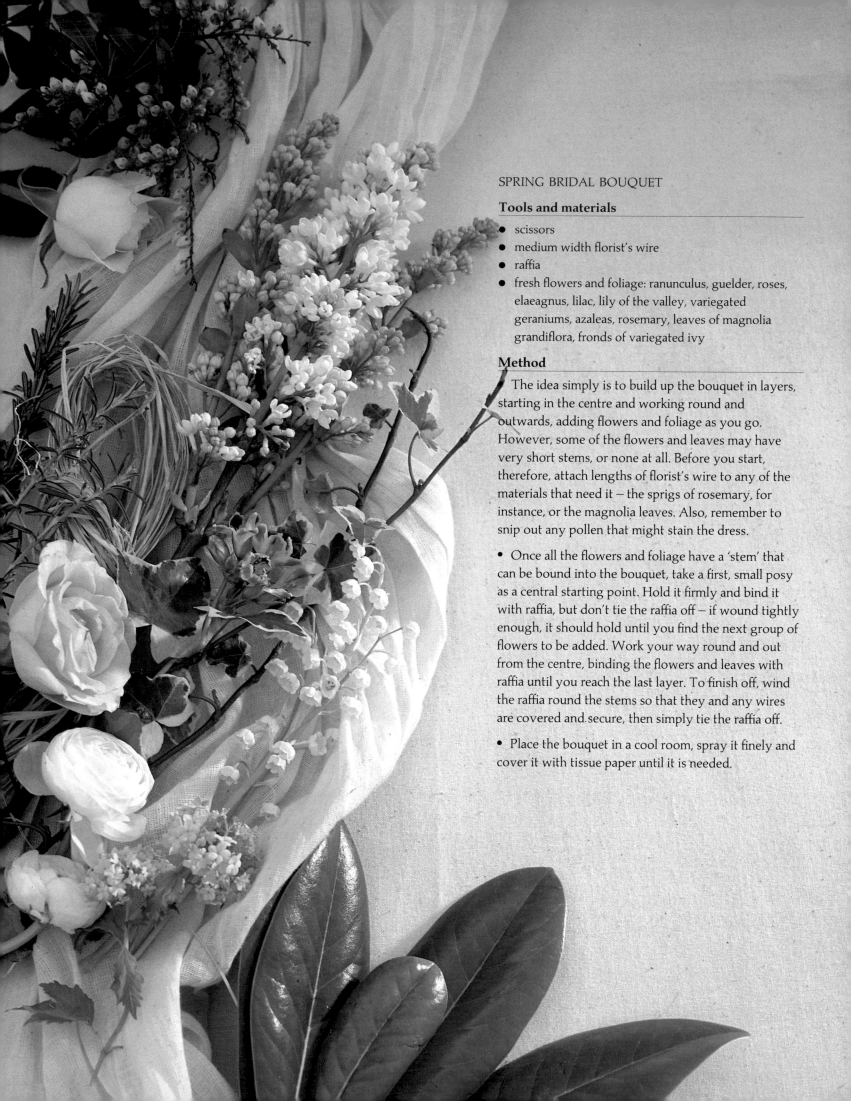

SPRING BRIDAL BOUQUET

Tools and materials

- scissors
- medium width florist's wire
- raffia
- fresh flowers and foliage: ranunculus, guelder, roses, elaeagnus, lilac, lily of the valley, variegated geraniums, azaleas, rosemary, leaves of magnolia grandiflora, fronds of variegated ivy

Method

The idea simply is to build up the bouquet in layers, starting in the centre and working round and outwards, adding flowers and foliage as you go. However, some of the flowers and leaves may have very short stems, or none at all. Before you start, therefore, attach lengths of florist's wire to any of the materials that need it — the sprigs of rosemary, for instance, or the magnolia leaves. Also, remember to snip out any pollen that might stain the dress.

• Once all the flowers and foliage have a 'stem' that can be bound into the bouquet, take a first, small posy as a central starting point. Hold it firmly and bind it with raffia, but don't tie the raffia off — if wound tightly enough, it should hold until you find the next group of flowers to be added. Work your way round and out from the centre, binding the flowers and leaves with raffia until you reach the last layer. To finish off, wind the raffia round the stems so that they and any wires are covered and secure, then simply tie the raffia off.

• Place the bouquet in a cool room, spray it finely and cover it with tissue paper until it is needed.

SPRING HAIR PIECE

Tools and materials

- scissors
- fine reel wire
- fine florist's wire
- Brown Guttacoll, or stemwind
- fresh flowers and foliage with short, 2–3-inch stems: ranunculus, lilies, feverfew, guelder, jasmine, rosemary

Method

• Bind several lengths of reel wire together with Guttacoll to make the hair piece's main support. The Guttacoll not only hides the wire, it also prevents it from rusting if the piece is sprayed and left for any time.

• Snip out the pollen as necessary and then wire the flowers either singly or in small bunches, depending on their size. Lilies, for instance, are best wired individually. Hold the flower gently by its head and insert a length of fine florist's wire at the top of the stem. Rotate the flower, winding the wire round and down as you go. Then cover the wire with Guttacoll, winding it round in the same way.

• Once all the flowers have been wired and their stems covered, arrange them along the main support until you are satisfied with the balance in colour, size and shape. Then, starting at one end of the hair piece wire, bind on each of the flowers or small bunches in turn with more Guttacoll.

• Once finished, the hair piece, like the bouquet, can be kept in a cool room, sprayed and covered with tissue paper until it is needed.

This striking bouquet of red and pink ranunculus, orange lilies, anemones tinged with pink, elaeagnus, rosemary and spring foliage is made in just the same way as described on p. 128, with a central posy bound with raffia, around which further flowers are added layer after layer to create a vibrant, secure display. The side hair piece includes ranunculus, guelder, anemones, lilies and rosemary, wired and bound with Guttacoll and attached to a short support, which is then pinned in place once the bride's hair has been styled.

Shells can be incorporated into hair pieces and bouquets as easily as they can into other decorations, and if they're used to complement the subtle sheen of a beaded satin dress, the effect can be stunning. For the bouquet, shells of various shapes and sizes are given a 'stem' by drilling two small holes near their base and wiring them up in the normal way. Here, they were then bound with raffia into a bouquet that also included white ranunculus and double tulips.

The hair piece is made from several pre-strung shell necklaces wound round and wired together into a cap. It would be best to make this and let the bride try it on before the day of the wedding so that when it comes to a final fitting, only minor adjustments should be needed.

Exquisitely simple dresses can be completely overpowered by large, traditional bouquets with the result that neither are seen to best effect. Far better to complement classic lines with bold but minimal decorations that are eye-catching but do not interfere. Here the long, graceful line of the dress is echoed by the stems and shapely heads of tall arum lilies, bound with nothing but twists of raffia.

Alternatively, the bouquet may be nothing more than the simplest of foliage posies, in this case, shamrock and camellia, bound with raffia. Pinned lightly but securely across the shoulders, however, is a cascading trail of stephanotis, the colours of its flowers and foliage complementing both the dress and posy without spoiling the simplicity of either.

I once heard of a bride to be who was determined to have a winter wedding because she wanted not a bouquet but a muff. In the event, she was married, complete with traditional bouquet, in mid-summer; but if she'd known, she could easily have what she originally wanted.

A **moss muff** (p. 136), decorated with seasonal flowers, is extremely straightforward to make and can add a stylish flourish to a host of different dresses. To complete the look, a moss hair piece also makes a change from a wired decoration.

● To make the hair piece, take a 1-inch wide length of thick ribbon, such as petersham, that will meet end to end around the bride's head.

● Attach short lengths of reel wire to each end to tie it together and then glue carpet moss to both sides, making sure it is completely covered.

● Once the moss band is tied in place, simply take one or two flowers of the kind that have been used to decorate the muff — in this case, lilies — wire the stems and cover with Guttacoll and then attach them to the back of the band where the edges meet.

Bouquets using materials in only one or two colours can often be as rich as those using an abundance of shades, especially if they incorporate a variety of shapes and textures.

Set against deep green box and encircled by a coil of galvanized wire, the unusual, pointed petals of the white horned tulips at the centre of the bouquet (p. 137) are displayed at their most dramatic. Equally powerful in its simplicity is the galvanized wire crown.

● *To make the latter, take a coil of fairly narrow galvanized wire and adjust it so that it will sit comfortably on the bride's head.*

● *Holding it to the correct diameter, unwind a couple of coils and then re-wind them, but twist them as you go into loops or points around the main ring, or crown base.*

● *Wind the end two or three times round the base to finish off.*

From the dramatic to the romantic. Bound into a bouquet layer by layer as before, these white double tulips, with their gently rounded shape and tissue-like, multi-layered petals are the perfect accompaniment for this sumptuously full dress and its flowered details.

MOSS MUFF

Tools and materials

- scissors
- glue gun
- fine reel wire
- florist's wire
- 12 × 18-inch piece of strong but flexible straw matting or card
- carpet moss
- fresh seasonal flowers

Method

• Lay the matting or card out flat and glue carpet moss to one side, leaving uncovered a ¾-inch strip along one of the shorter edges.

• With the moss on the inside, roll up the matting or card and join the shorter edges together, gluing the ¾-inch strip to what is now the outer side and making sure the moss meets edge to edge underneath.

• Glue carpet moss to the outside of the roll until it is completely covered.

• Take a length of florist's wire and push both its ends, about 2 inches apart, through the muff from the underside. Twist the wire ends into a loose loop and insert the flowers, pressing the wire down to keep them in place.

If you want to add more flowers than the loop can safely hold, either trim their stems and attach them with fine reel wire to stalks already held in place, or make a further loop of florist's wire and tie them in as above.

BOUQUET OF BOX, TULIPS AND GALVANIZED WIRE

Tools and materials

- scissors
- florist's wire
- coil of galvanized wire
- sprigs of box
- white horned tulips
- raffia

Method

- Take the galvanized wire coil and bind three or four lengths of florist's wire together at three points on its circumference – two opposite each other, the third an equal distance between. Pull the loose wire ends together and twist into a stalk in the centre of the ring.

- Wire together sprigs of box into dense clusters (see p. 26).

- Holding the galvanized wire by its central stalk, feed a small bunch of tulips through the hole and bind them to the wire stalk with raffia. Build up the bouquet in the normal way, binding in layer after layer of tulips until you reach the inside edge of the galvanized coil. Thereafter, bind in the wired box sprigs, bending them so that they sit under the coil rather than on top of it.

- When the coil and tulips are completely encircled by box, securely fasten off the raffia, making sure that all sharp wire ends are covered to prevent them damaging the dress.

- Trim any wayward ends of box, spray the tulips with water, cover with tissue paper and keep somewhere cool until needed.

137

CHRISTMAS

Christmas seems to arrive earlier and earlier with every year that passes. Now, as soon as the summer holidays are over, tinsel and cards can be found filling shop floors where the garden furniture used to be and, as the autumn goes by, we are constantly reminded how few days we have left to prepare for the festivities. The build-up is often so long that by the time the true festive season does arrive, all the magic has gone; the real reason for the celebration has been smothered in swathes of tinsel and glitter.

I'm not pretending I can ignore all this preparation: the weeks leading up to Christmas are one of my busiest periods, when I create seasonal decorations of all sizes for clients and for the shop. I do try, though, to keep the magic of Christmas in mind, which means that I ignore the tinsel and baubles. For me, Christmas is best conjured up by a basket of cones and nuts on a table; a wreath of berries and fruits to welcome people at the door; a garland of cinnamon sticks and candles hanging by the fire, filling the room with warm colour and fragrance. Christmas should be a time to relax and reflect, and I can think of no more appropriate a way to do so than to fill a home with natural, seasonal decorations.

SOME SEASONAL INGREDIENTS AND THEIR USES

Cinnamon sticks bind five or six together with wire and insert in garlands, wreaths and basket decorations

Christmas roses these make very attractive, delicate table decorations, either on their own in a pot or basket, or as part of a larger display

eucalyptus I love the silvery green foliage and potent scent of this plant and incorporate it in decorations all year round. At Christmas, I use it to add body and texture to garlands and wreaths

evergreens the deep green foliage of pines, juniper, spruce and boxwood give body, shape and texture to substantial displays

fir cones wire up singly or in groups of two or three and add to garlands, wreaths, baskets and candlestands

gourds these provide vibrant splashes of colour when wired into displays of all kinds; their unusual shapes add a natural quirkiness that catches the eye.

holly the dark green, shiny leaves provide body, shape and texture for garlands and wreaths, while the deep red berries add warm dashes of colour

ivy trailing fronds of ivy add all-important movement to garlands and wreaths, and I'm especially fond of the variegated types because of their subtle colouring

larch the delicate, frond-like twigs with their tiny cones give a natural height or breadth to basket decorations, wreaths and garlands. They are particularly attractive when covered in lichen

mistletoe a firm favourite, this is ideal for wreaths or garlands

nuts walnuts, hazelnuts, monkey nuts or chestnuts can be used in decorations of all sizes. Try varnishing chestnuts and wiring them into a basket display; or tying walnuts into a garland, where their colour, shape and texture will contrast wonderfully with the evergreen foliage

poinsettia this is one of the few fresh flowers used during the festive season, and will add eye-catching bursts of red or pink to large displays

ABOVE *A **basket of hyacinths** (p. 140). Pine cones, nuts, apples and sweet-smelling cinnamon sticks arranged together conjure up the festive season to perfection. This basket, however, with its fresh hyacinths, will last long past Christmas — a comforting reminder of the old year and a promise of the new.*

OPPOSITE *For me, this rich profusion of natural colours and scents conjures up what Christmas is all about. I know of nothing more conducive to relaxed contemplation at this special time of year than the warm glow of candles, the deep greens of pine or spruce, nuts in all their varied shapes and textures and the fragrance of spices.*

A BASKET OF HYACINTHS

Tools and materials

- scissors
- bradawl
- basket
- piece of polythene to line the basket
- plastic bowl that fits snugly inside the basket
- florist's wire
- carpet moss
- house plant compost
- hyacinth bulbs that have already begun to shoot
- red apples
- fir cones — if you want to cover the basket sides with them, make sure you have enough to do so; if you simply want to arrange them round the hyacinths, you'll need only a handful
- cinnamon sticks
- 10-inch lengths of raffia or rough string
- nuts — walnuts, chestnuts or hazelnuts are ideal
- larch fronds, each 6—8 inches long

Method

• If you are decorating the basket with cones, wire them one by one to the wickerwork (see p. 23), making sure the entire area is evenly covered.

• Line the basket with the polythene (see p. 23) and place the plastic bowl inside.

• Wire up the cones, apples and nuts (see p. 26).

• Bind the cinnamon sticks with wire into bundles of 6, leaving a length of wire long enough to attach each bundle to the decoration. Then conceal the binding with a length of raffia or rough string.

• Fill the bowl with compost to within an inch of the top, plant the hyacinths and then cover the exposed soil with moss, making sure that it also hides the rim of the container and any of the polythene lining that may still be visible.

• Take the wired apples, cones, nuts and cinnamon stick bundles and push their wires through the moss and into the soil until the surface is covered and the hyacinths are nestling in a warm bed of rich, natural scent and colour. Lastly, arrange the larch fronds amongst the other ingredients — their height will form a natural backdrop for the hyacinths as they grow.

In addition to the seasonal materials listed above, there is, of course, a limitless range of non-seasonal (and by this I mean season-less, rather than out-of-season) ingredients that can be used to create natural yet festive decorations. Richly coloured dried flowers add warmth when set against evergreen foliage; bundles of dried lavender tied into a garland will fill a room with their heady fragrance; dried citrus fruits make an unusual addition to a candlestand or table decoration. And don't forget the fresh fruit: rosy red or russet apples, oranges, lemons and pomegranates look superb when wired into decorations of all sizes. Finally, remember that baskets and pots are not just for holding a display – they can be added in just the same way as a cone or an apple. If a small basket or interestingly shaped piece of terracotta pot looks as if it ought to belong to a garland or wreath, wire it in!

'Traditional' Christmas wreaths (p. 144), for example, can be filled to bursting not just with seasonal materials but also with birch poles whose fate might otherwise have been to be covered as a candlestand, small terracotta pots found at the back of the shelf or shed, and red apples that you can find in the supermarket every day of the year.

DECORATING THE CHRISTMAS TREE

Covering the tree with materials such as those described above not only looks more natural, it can also be great fun, particularly for children, if it means making small decorations. Let them fill small terracotta pots with fir cones or cinnamon sticks tied into bundles, which can then be wired onto some of the tree's lower, sturdier branches. Or show them how to make the dried rose balls pictured here.

● All you'll need are small oasis or dry

sack moss and wire balls, short lengths of decorative cord with wires at each end, handfuls of dried rose heads with 2-inch stalks and a little glue.

● First, attach the cord loop to the ball, pushing in its wires as far as they'll go and then gluing the tips of the cord to the ball's surface to hold it in place.

● Then, working systematically round the mould, insert the roses by their stalks, packing them together until the area is

completely covered.

You can use any variety of small, dried flower or fresh flowers that will dry as they hang. Alternatively, you can simply glue carpet moss all over the ball for a rich, velvety effect.

Instead of the traditional glittering star at the top of the tree, you might make a birch bow.

● Take a handful of supple birch branches, trim them to the same length

and lay them in a strip on a flat surface.

● Pull the ends over to make two loops of the same size, binding the branches in the centre where they cross.

● Attach a length of florist's wire to the back of the bow and bind it to the top of the tree, where its subtle, natural shades and texture can be picked out by small, candlelike tree lights.

RIBBONED WREATH

Tools and materials

- scissors
- bradawl
- drill with $\frac{1}{4}$-inch bit
- florist's large wire wreath frame
- stub wire or hair pins
- reel wire
- florist's wire
- galvanized wire
- dry sack moss
- polythene sheet to back wreath
- clear varnish (optional)
- small varnishing brush (optional)
- red apples

- cinnamon sticks
- birch poles, each about 5 inches long
- fir cones
- small terracotta pots
- walnuts
- chestnuts
- bunches of dried lavender
- sprigs of spruce or fir
- larch fronds
- small sprigs of cotoneaster berries
- raffia
- lengths of rough string or rope
- 36-inch length of 4-inch-wide decorative ribbon

Method

- Prepare the wreath frame. Attach reel wire to a point

on the circumference, take a handful of moss and, holding it round the frame, bind it securely in place. Continue until the entire frame is covered with a thick but firm moss blanket.

• Wire up the nuts (see p. 26) and group them in clusters of 3 to 5. Varnish the chestnuts if desired and leave to dry. Wire the fir cones in groups of 3, the red apples singly, the lavender and cotoneaster in small bunches and sprigs.

• Bind the cinnamon sticks with wire into bundles of 8 and then conceal the binding with raffia. Tie the birch poles together in pairs with the rough string or rope and wrap a couple of lengths of florist's wire through and round the rope to form a stalk. Then wire up the small terracotta pots (see p. 27).

• Begin decorating the wreath by inserting the spruce or fir to give background colour and texture. Then wire in the nuts, fir cones, apples, lavender, cotoneaster, cinnamon stick bundles, birch poles and pots until the wreath is covered in a profusion of different colours, scents and shapes. Finally, insert the larch fronds as a final, natural flourish.

• Cut the ribbon into two pieces, one 24 inches the other 12 inches long. Tie each into a separate bow and then wire the smaller one to the front of the larger. Attach this double-bow to the wreath with another length of wire.

• Lastly, pin the protective polythene backing to the wreath, attach the ends of a length of strong wire to two points on the frame's circumference, and hang.

As an alternative to the traditional tree, these topiary orange trees (see pp. 148–9) and box-covered basket piled high with fruit make a magnificent, warming display full of vibrant colours and seasonal cheer. They would also make a stunning centrepiece for a large Christmas party.

● To cover and fill the basket you will need 2-inch wire netting, dry sack moss, and plentiful quantities of box and fruit.

● If the basket does not already have a handle one can easily be made by setting a tall arch of birch branches inside the basket and binding the ends to the wickerwork.

● To cover the basket and handle, wrap lightly scrunched wire netting around the outsides of both, knitting the wire edges together and binding in any loose ends to hold it firmly in place. You might also attach the netting to the basket rim using short lengths of florist's or stub wire so that it won't sag when the box is inserted.

● Push short pieces of box through the netting all round the basket and handle until they are completely covered; then trim the ends of the box for a sculpted, topiary effect.

● Make a dry sack moss and wire mould that will almost fill the basket and, once in position, shape it into a firm, even mound to support the fruit.

● Use as many kinds of fruit as you can find – pineapples, pomegranates, apples, bananas, grapes, lychees, melons, pears, strawberries, peaches. Wire up the larger pieces individually and set the smaller, softer fruits, such as the strawberries and lychees, into their own baskets. Then insert the fruits and baskets into the mould, piling them high and letting them 'tumble' over the main basket rim in a display of true natural abundance.

TOPIARY ORANGE TREE

Tools and materials (for one tree)

- scissors
- staple gun
- large, deep plastic bowl or bucket
- sturdy pole cut to the height you wish your tree to be — those illustrated here were about 5 feet tall, but they can be much smaller as long as they're kept in proportion
- finishing plaster or light cement
- 6 × 8-inch lengths of bamboo or $\frac{1}{2}$-inch dowling
- wire wreath frame
- 2-inch wire netting
- florist's wire
- dry sack moss
- box branches
- oranges
- 8 × 12-inch long, $1\frac{1}{2}$-inch diameter candles

Method

• Prepare the pole and bucket as you would a birch pole stand (see p.20). The pole should reach to the bucket's base; the bucket itself should be filled three-quarters full of plaster or cement so that the whole tree will stand absolutely steady.

• Lightly scrunch a length of wire netting and then wrap it around the outside of the bucket so that it fits snugly but not too tightly. Knit the edges together and turn in any loose, sharp ends.

• Take small clumps of sack moss and push them through the netting round the bucket until it is completely covered with a thick, firm moss blanket.

• Prepare the pole. Take a large piece of wire netting and scrunch it into a long mould. Wrap the mould

around the pole so that it reaches down to the cement and stands taller than the pole end by 3 or 4 inches. Staple the netting to the pole in several places so that it is held securely and there are no loose edges or sharp ends. Then fill the mould with sack moss, pushing it through the netting until you have a firm, evenly shaped pillar.

• Take the wire wreath frame and fill the core with wire netting, bent and moulded so that it will support the box when inserted. Then place the frame round the central moss mould, about a third of the way up from the base.

• Make the second wire ring by winding a length of firmly crumpled netting around the central mould and knitting the ends together. When positioning these rings, make sure above all that the candles of the lower frame, when wired in, will stand clear of the top ring, out of the way of any foliage.

• Secure the frames in position by driving the bamboo canes or dowling at regular intervals through the netting and into the central moss mould.

• Wire up the oranges individually — the most time-consuming task, which can be done in stages, particularly if you're not sure how many oranges you'll need.

• Make the box base by inserting short branches of box into the moss and wire blanket round the bucket, making sure the whole area is evenly and densely covered. Trim the branches, cutting a little at a time and working round systematically for an even, symmetrical shape.

• Next, wire oranges into the moss and wire mould between the base and first wire frame, working round in rows until the area is completely covered.

• Insert short box branches into the wreath frame and netting. Trim the top of the frame flat and shape the sides so that they taper towards the oranges below to create a truly sculpted effect.

• Cover the central mould between the two frames with more wired oranges and then make the second box wreath in just the same way as the first.

• Wire in the last oranges to the top of the mould.

• As a final flourish, make a small wire netting ball, cover it with box as above and trim. Wire it to the top of the tree with florist's wire.

• Take each of the candles and wrap two or three lengths of florist's wire securely around the base of each. Then arrange them at regular intervals around the box rings, pushing their wires right in so that they stand rigid — and straight.

A CHRISTMAS COLLECTION

Two or three of these **fruit and nut candlestands** (p. 154) would make wonderfully rich and warming decorations for a Christmas dinner party. Place them down the centre of the table and between them, for contrast, set shallow baskets or trays piled high with walnuts, hazelnuts and chestnuts.

This **dried citrus pot** (p. 152), with its textured slices of dried grapefruit, and vibrant dried peppers and flowers, makes a striking centrepiece for a small table. As with the box

and fruit basket described above and, indeed, with any abundant display, the materials should be wired in to overflowing, as if one breath would send the carefully balanced mound tumbling.

A cone and cinnamon garland (p. 153) hung in a hallway or beside the fire is much more welcoming than any tinsel. It can be made to any length you like, but I'd suggest, given the individual pieces of rosemary and larch will be at least 12 inches long, that it be a minimum of 5 feet to keep it in proportion.

DRIED CITRUS POT

Tools and materials

- scissors
- glue gun
- medium-sized terracotta pot
- 2-inch wire netting
- florist's wire
- dry sack moss
- dried poppy heads with 3-inch stems
- dried grapefruit slices
- strings of dried peppers
- dried flowers – here I used dahlias, but the choice is yours – red roses or hydrangeas, for instance, are particularly rich and attractive
- artificial strawberries (optional)

Method

• Fill the pot with a moss and wire mould (see p. 24), making a dome that stands as high again as the pot.

• Wire up the ingredients: the grapefruit slices in clusters of 5 or 6; the poppy heads in groups of 3; the flowers in posies of 3 to 5, depending on their size.

• Insert the wired grapefruit slices, poppy heads and flowers into the moss dome, making sure that the whole area is covered and that the ingredients are allowed to hand naturally over the pot's rim. Glue on the strawberries and, as a final splash of colour, drape lengths of pepper string around the grapefruit slices.

CONE AND CINNAMON GARLAND

Tools and materials

- scissors
- 2-inch wire netting
- stub wire or hair pins
- florist's wire
- dry sack moss
- polythene sheeting to back garland
- cinnamon sticks
- apples
- fir cones
- larch branches with cones or covered in lichen
- branches of spruce or fir
- fresh rosemary
- cotoneaster

Method

• Prepare the moss and wire garland support (see p.24).

• Bind the cinnamon sticks with wire into bundles of 6 or 7, leaving a length of wire long enough to attach each bundle to the garland. Then conceal the binding with a length of raffia or rough string.

• Wire up the apples and fir cones individually (see p.26).

• Insert the fronds of larch, spruce or fir and rosemary into the garland to form a rich, textured background, allowing them to hang down to give a natural-looking, feathered effect with plenty of movement.

• Then insert the cotoneaster and wire in the apples, grouping them to give bursts of colour and interspersing them with the fir cones and cinnamon stick bundles.

• Finally, attach the protective polythene sheet to the back of the garland with stub wire or hair pins (see p.24).

153

FRUIT AND NUT CANDLESTAND

Tools and materials

- scissors
- bradawl
- 1 large and 1 medium-sized terracotta pot
- bamboo cane
- reel wire
- florist's wire
- dry sack moss
- carpet moss
- sprigs of spruce or fir
- red or russet apples

- fir cones
- walnuts
- sprigs of cotoneaster berries
- cinnamon sticks
- raffia
- thick candle to fit snugly in the top of the smaller pot

Method

• Fill the larger terracotta pot with sack moss until three-quarters full. Insert the bamboo cane into the moss in the centre of the pot until it reaches the pot base. Place the smaller pot on top, so that it sits firmly on the moss and the bamboo cane comes through its

drainage hole. Trim the cane so that it reaches about halfway up the inside of the smaller pot, then fill this pot with sack moss to the rim.

• Cover the larger pot with sack moss. Wind reel wire round the pot's rim, take a handful of moss and, holding it against the pot, bind it in place. Continue until the whole of the pot is covered with a thick, firm layer of moss and tie the wire off.

• Wire up the walnuts in groups of 3, the apples and fir cones individually.

• Bind the cinnamon sticks into bundles of 8 and then conceal the binding with raffia.

• Starting at the base of the large pot, insert the sprigs of fir or spruce into the moss all the way round. Then build up layers above, wiring in the cinnamon stick bundles, cones, nuts, cotoneaster sprigs and apples until the pot is covered. Finish with a row of apples wired into the sack moss inside the pot.

• Lastly, wedge the candle firmly into the moss in the smaller pot and wrap its base with carpet moss.

TOOLS AND ACCESSORIES

The list below includes implements and materials I always have to hand when I'm working. Some of the items, such as the drill, I don't use every day, but there's nothing more infuriating than not having one when it's needed. My scissors, however, I carry in my back pocket all the time. To lose them would be like a painter losing his favourite brush and each of us in the studio has our own, carefully identified pair.

All the items below can be readily obtained from a florist's, garden centre or hardware store.

TOOLS

- pair of florist's scissors (ordinary, household scissors won't do as they're not robust enough and their blades are too long)
- pliers
- bradawl
- garden shears
- staple gun
- hand or electric saw
- drill with bits of various sizes

ACCESSORIES

- 2-inch wire netting
- stub wire (hair pins are a good alternative, or you can cut florist's wire into short pieces)
- reel wire
- florist's wire
- galvanized wire
- screws
- nuts
- rubber gloves (useful for jobs that involve glue, such as sticking carpet moss to a sack moss and wire mould or birch bow)
- glue stick or gun
- Oasis Fix
- Guttacoll, or stemwind, for bridal flowers

- finishing plaster or light cement
- garden string
- bamboo canes
- watering can
- water-resistant adhesive tape
- polythene sheeting or plastic bin liners
- plastic buckets
- plastic bowls
- plastic tubes or extenders for holding fresh displays
- oasis rings

- small, medium, large terracotta pots
- small, medium, large baskets

- house plant compost
- birch poles
- sack moss
- carpet moss

- raffia
- hessian
- rough string and rope

ACKNOWLEDGEMENTS

This book would not have been possible without the support and hard work of numerous friends and colleagues. I am indebted, above all, to my special team: Bronwen Careless, Alison Wakelin, Sophie Berthier, Roger Street, John Lewis, Julie Thompson, Michael Walter, Benedikt Humm, June Strong, Harald Altmayer and Peter Le Cren. I am also deeply grateful to photographer Marie-Louise Avery and my editor, Lesley Baxter.

I extend special thanks to my partners in Japan: Mr Shibata, Ms Yumi Kaitoh, Mr Nishimura, Ms Mieko Shimizu, Ms Emiko Takahashi, and all of the Kenneth Turner team in Tokyo.

In addition, the publishers and I would like to thank:
Mrs Alaghband
Jacqueline Borgust
Dr Boss
Clifton Little Venice Ltd
Christine Corson
Mrs D. Crutchley
The Dorchester Hotel
Michael Edser
Mr and Mrs Gertler
Thomas Goode
Kiloran Howard
Caron Keating
Mrs Lemos
Joseph Levin, The Greenhouse Restaurant, Mayfair
Mr and Mrs Levin, Capitol Hotel
Sarah McAlpine
John Miller
The Monogram Linen Shop
Peter's Posh Pets
The Royal Academy
Paul Ryan
J. Sainsbury plc
Michael and Fiona Savory
Mr and Mrs Stottart (dog-minding)

Jill Strieder
Catherine Walker Bridalwear

and, from Covent Garden market:

Martin and Terry, Arnott & Mason
Dennis, John Austin
David Bacon
Kenneth, Bates
Danny Cole and Son
John and David Egan
Charlie Gardiner
Peter and Ron Hardcastle
Victor and Colin, KSM
Lyons & Dean
Lionel Mills
Charlie and Brian Porter
Quality Plants
and not forgetting my porter, Roy Steptoe

The very idea of this, the second book, however, would not have been feasible but for the unfailing enthusiasm and support over the years of many companies, institutions and individuals, to whom is due, in large part, the success of my work and business.

My personal thanks go especially to:
Mrs Alaghband
Mrs Al-Turki
Lady Amphill
Lady Elizabeth Anson
Mr and Mrs Arida
Giorgio Armani
Lauren Bacall
Sir Anthony and Lady Bamford
Baroness Bentinck
Paolo Biscioni
Jacqueline Blanc
Godfrey and Susan Bradman
Rose-Marie Bravo
His Excellency, the Brazilian Ambassador, Senhor Paulo Tarso Flecha de Lima and Madame Lucia Flecha de Lima

Sally Burton
George Cameron-Nash
Mr and Mrs Chatwell
Lindka Cierach
Joan Collins
Neville and Carol Conrad
Fleur Cowles
Duchesse De Cadaval
Mrs Yolanda de Fierro
Mr Pietro de Panizza
Baron de Rede
Mr and Mrs Druion
Martine Dulles
Mr and Mrs Esfandi
Carlo Fachetti
Fenwick of Bond St
HRH The Princess Firyal of Jordan
Mrs Fitzgibbon
Mrs Geni Rudolf Flick
Forte UK Limited
Fortnum and Mason
Princess Ira von Furstenburg
Susan Gutfreund
Mr and Mrs D. Goulandris
Mr and Mrs G. Goulandris
Guilda Gourlay
Rod and Jenny Hall
Mrs Hambro
Susan Hampshire

OPPOSITE *Proving that baskets are not just for holding decorations, this life-size character stands at the entrance of a client's restaurant.*

PAGE 1 *I was asked to create a frame for the book's dust jacket, an invitation I just couldn't refuse.*

PAGE 2 *At home with my two faithful companions, Bumble and Murphy.*

DEDICATION *A celebration of nature's Autumn riches.*

PAGE 6 *The Dorchester Hotel, London, transformed into a woodland glade for a client's wedding.*

The Princess of Hanover
Pamela, Lady Harlech
George and Olivia Harrison
Harrods
Harvey Nichols
Mrs Hazandrous
Drew Heinz
Will and Jill Hollinger
David and Stormy Hull
Gloria Hunniford
Angus and Joyce James
Sally James
JRB Associates
HRH the Princess Michael of Kent
Mr and Mrs Kouzor
Ginette and Paul Lambert
Mr Edward Leaman
Mr and Mrs Lemos
Lady Lever
Gemma Levine
Sarah McAlpine
Paul and Bunny Mellon
Anton Mosimann
Ginger Nash
Don Norton
Mr and Mrs Nabil Obayda
Tony Page
Tom Parr
Claudine Pereira
Mrs Louisa Pipe
Earl and Countess of Plymouth
Linda Rhodes
Gail Ronson
Johnny Roxborough
Maurice and Charles Saatchi
Mortimer and Theresa Sackler
Lily Saffra
Mr and Mrs Salzburger
Michael and Fiona Savory
Selfridges Ltd
Mr and Mrs Seymour
His Excellency Ghassan Shaker
Belle Shenkman-Smith
Lord Snowdon
Scott Snyder
Angela Sonning
Raine, Countess Spencer

The Honourable Mr Justice Stone and
   Mrs Stone
Lord and Lady Tanlaw
Mr and Mrs Alfred Taubman
Mr and Mrs Townsley
Ivana Trump
Mr and Mrs Yacobi Strasser
Mr and Mrs Victor Ward
Lady Weinberg
Lady Weinstock
Mark Williams

PHOTOGRAPHIC ACKNOWLEDGEMENTS

All the photographs were specially commissioned by Weidenfeld and Nicolson from Marie-Louise Avery with the exception of the following which were taken by:
John Miller 46–7, 55 top and bottom left, 61, 68–9, 70, 71, 76–7, 90–1, 92, 93, 117, 123, 158
Kiloran Howard 5, 12–13, 112 left, 113, 116, 120, 121, 122, 124 bottom, 156
Lesley Baxter, 112 middle and right
Ian Macauly 114